Life Skills 101:

The Crash Course in Adulting - Because Apparently You Should Know This By Now

BY
ROSE LYONS

Contents

Introduction

"Success is not final, failure is not fatal: It is the courage to continue that counts."

—Winston Churchill

Ever feel like adulting is a wild rollercoaster ride with no seatbelts? Welcome to the not-so-secret club of young adulthood! Life's a blend of epic adventures and bewildering mazes. But fear not, this guide is your treasure map, helping you navigate health, wealth, relationships, and self-care like a pro. Get ready to conquer the adulting maze with style!

Think of this guide as a friendly chat about everything you're supposed to know as an adult but maybe no one thought to teach you along the way. We're talking about the nitty-gritty of managing healthcare – that includes understanding appropriate social etiquette especially in group settings or traveling. These are situations you are less likely to have encountered while in high school. And then there's the whole world of learning how to manage your finances to be prepared for whatever situation that life will put you in. We've got you.

But it's not all paperwork and health jargon. Life's also about the connections you make and the relationships you build. This book dives into the art of safely dating (offline and online), maintaining healthy relationships, and even getting a grip on sexual health education – because it's a big part of life.

And then there's money - the root of so much adulting stress. We'll walk you through budgeting, managing your finances, and even the ins and outs of side hustles. Because who doesn't want a little extra cash?

Living on your own is another big leap. Whether finding your place, whipping up a decent meal, or figuring out how to do laundry without calling home, we cover the essentials of independent living. And let's not forget about the digital world we're living in. Your online life, from social media to digital literacy, is as real as your offline one. Navigating it safely and smartly is key.

Most importantly, we're here to talk about mental health and well-being. Taking care of your mind is as important as caring for your body. Understanding mental health, developing coping strategies, and knowing when and how to seek help is vital.

This guide is about getting you equipped with the skills and knowledge to live your best life. It's casual, straightforward, and hopefully, a bit fun. So, let's dive into these pages and uncover the secrets to navigating your early twenties with confidence and a bit of flair.

CHAPTER 1

Healthcare 101

E ver wondered why adulting doesn't come with an instruction manual? Well, here's a question for you: Do you know how to navigate the healthcare maze as a savvy consumer? This chapter is your backstage pass to understanding the ins and outs of healthcare in the real world, where you're not just the patient but also the decision-maker. As you navigate the exciting path of independence, you might encounter various healthcare challenges, from deciphering insurance plans to making appointments and managing prescriptions. You're not alone in facing these uncertainties, and this chapter is here to demystify healthcare, empower you with knowledge, and help you make informed decisions about your well-being. So, let's dive in and unravel the intricacies of healthcare, ensuring that you're well-prepared to take charge of your health and make the best choices for your future. To begin our exploration of this chapter, let's start by clarifying some important terminology. This will provide you with a solid foundation and make it easier to grasp the concepts discussed in the upcoming sections.

Healthcare Terminology Explained

Premium: This is the regular payment you make to your health insurance company. Many individuals receive insurance coverage through their employers, with the premium automatically deducted from their paychecks. Alternatively, some individuals choose to purchase insurance independently, paying for it directly rather than going through their employer.

Deductible: The initial amount you must pay out of your pocket for covered healthcare services before your insurance starts covering costs. This does not mean you pay the full cost but instead you pay the contractual rate that the physician, practice or hospital has agreed to with the insurance company.

Co-pay (Co-payment): A fixed amount you pay for a specific healthcare service or prescription, often due at the time of service.

Co-insurance: The percentage of healthcare costs you share with your insurance company after you've met your deductible. Typically this is 80/20 or 90/10. Again, this is based on the contractual rate the physician, practice or hospital has agreed to with the insurance company.

Out-of-Pocket Maximum (OOPM): You must pay for covered services in a plan year, including deductibles, co-pays, and co-insurance. Once you reach this limit, your insurance covers all additional costs.

In-Network: Healthcare providers and facilities that have a contract with your insurance company to provide services at pre-negotiated rates. Visiting in-network providers typically costs less.

Out-of-Network: Healthcare providers and facilities that do not have a contract with your insurance company. Visiting out-of-network providers often results in higher costs for you.

Preventive Care: Services such as vaccinations and screenings that aim to prevent health issues before they occur. Many insurance plans cover preventive care at no cost to the insured.

Emergency Care: Immediate medical treatment for severe or life-threatening conditions, often covered by insurance even if the provider is out-of-network. This is typically only seen at hospitals such as the ER.

Primary Care Physician (PCP): is like your healthcare quarterback, a central figure in your medical journey. They offer general medical care, serve as your first point of contact for health issues, and play a vital role in preventive care. Many health insurance plans also require you to have a designated PCP to streamline your healthcare management.

Specialist: A doctor with expertise in a specific area of medicine, such as a cardiologist, dermatologist, or orthopedist.

Prescription Drug Coverage: Insurance coverage for medications may involve co-pays or co-insurance for each prescription.

Health Savings Account (HSA): A tax-advantaged savings account paired with a high-deductible health plan used to save money for medical expenses.

Flexible Spending Account (FSA): A pre-tax savings account for medical expenses, often offered through your employer.

Explanation of Benefits (EOB): A document from your insurance company that explains how a claim was processed, including what they paid and what you owe.

Open Enrollment: A specific period during which you can sign up for or change your health insurance plan, usually once a year.

Dependent Coverage: The option to include family members, such as children or spouses, under your health insurance policy.

Authorization: Approval from your insurer or provider before specific medical services, which is vital to ensure your insurance covers the service and prevents unexpected expenses.

Referral: A recommendation from your primary care physician to see a specialist for a specific medical issue, ensuring you get appropriate care from an expert in that area.

In simple terms, processing claims in healthcare works like this:

- You receive medical care.
- The healthcare provider sends a bill to your insurance company, detailing the services provided.
- Your insurance company reviews the bill and determines what expenses they'll cover based on your policy.
- You may need to pay any costs not covered by your insurance, known as "out-of-pocket expenses."
- You will receive a bill from the provider to let you know how much you owe
  - You will receive a copy of the explanation of benefits from your insurance so be sure to match up your EOB with the bill from the provider to ensure there are no discrepancies

Healthcare Insurance

Understanding health insurance policies requires careful consideration of their costs, coverage, and healthcare provider selection process. Each plan offers a different balance of these elements, and choosing the right one depends heavily on your individual or family needs. It's crucial to review each policy thoroughly to determine which aligns best with your specific circumstances, even if you're still on your parents' coverage due to your age, you should understand the coverage to ensure you take appropriate steps to stay within the plan coverage.

When evaluating health plans, consider how frequently you or your family need medical care. If you have ongoing medical conditions or expect regular doctor visits, a plan with lower co-pays and a broad network of providers might be more beneficial despite potentially higher premiums. On the other hand, if you're generally healthy and seldom visit the doctor, a plan with lower monthly premiums but higher out-of-pocket costs for occasional care could be a more cost-effective choice.

Consider the immediate cost of premiums and how much you'd potentially pay out-of-pocket for services like specialist visits, prescriptions, and emergency care. Some plans may offer lower premiums but have higher deductibles and co-pays, which could cost more if you require frequent medical attention.

Additionally, think about the network of providers each plan offers. If you have preferred doctors or specialists, ensure they are included in the plan's network. If not, you might have to pay more to see out-of-network providers or choose a different plan altogether.

Lastly, consider any specific health needs you or your family may have. For example, if someone requires regular specialist care, mental health services, or maternity care, ensure the plan covers these adequately.

In summary, selecting the right health insurance policy balances cost, coverage, and convenience. It's vital to assess your personal and family health needs carefully and compare them against what each plan offers to make an informed decision that provides the best possible coverage for your situation.

Six Most Common Insurance Plans

HMOs (Health Maintenance Organizations):

- ▸ Limit coverage to network providers except in emergencies.
- ▸ Require primary care physician (PCP) referrals.
- ▸ Offer lower monthly rates and typically lower cost-sharing (deductibles, co-pays, out-of-pocket maximums) compared to PPOs, especially in employer-provided plans.
- ▸ Individual HMO plans may have out-of-pocket costs comparable to PPOs.

PPOs (Preferred Provider Organizations):

- ▸ Provide a preferred provider network but also cover out-of-network care.
- ▸ Feature higher monthly premiums and cost-sharing due to less restrictive networks.
- ▸ Have seen a decline in popularity as networks shrink and shift to EPOs and HMOs.
- ▸ Predominant in employer-sponsored plans but less common in individual markets, with some states no longer offering them.

EPOs (Exclusive Provider Organizations):

- ▸ Operate with a specific provider network and don't cover out-of-network care except in emergencies.
- ▸ Do not typically require a PCP referral for specialists.
- ▸ Function like PPOs but without out-of-network coverage.

POS (Point of Service) Plans:

- ▸ Blend features of HMOs and PPOs.
- ▸ Allow some out-of-network care under certain conditions.
- ▸ Often require PCP referrals for all medical services.

Indemnity Plans:

- ▸ Offer traditional fee-for-service coverage without managed care.

- ▸ Reimburse a percentage of charges for covered medical procedures.
- ▸ Have become rare in modern healthcare, with less than 1% of American workers with employer-sponsored health coverage using them.
- ▸ Most current medical policies offer managed care, though dental indemnity plans are still common.

HSA (Health Savings Accounts):

- ▸ It is not a specific type of managed care but can be used with various plans like HMOs, PPOs, EPOs, and POS.
- ▸ Must adhere to IRS guidelines on plan design.

The Significance of Health Insurance and What It Encompasses

In simple terms, health insurance is your financial safety net in the unpredictable world of healthcare. It's like having a friend who's got your back when you least expect it. So, why is it such a big deal, especially for a young adult like you? Let's break it down.

Financial Safety Net: Think of health insurance as your superhero cape for medical expenses. It's a legal agreement between you and an insurance company that steps in to cover the costs when you're hit with unexpected medical bills. Whether it's an illness, an accident, or any other covered event, health insurance ensures you're not drowning in medical debt.

Insurance Processing Methods: When it comes to paying your medical bills, your health insurance company does it in two ways:

- ▸ **In-Network Care:** If you seek treatment at a hospital or with doctors within your insurance network, you usually don't have to dig into your pockets during service. Your health plan takes care of the bills directly.
- ▸ **Out-of-Pocket Costs:** If you receive care outside of your network, you might need to pay some costs upfront, but you can later request reimbursement from your insurance provider.

Why It Matters – The Consequences of Going Without Health Insurance

While having health insurance offers a safety net, it's equally important to understand the potential downsides of not having coverage. Here's a glimpse into what could happen if you decide to go without health insurance:

Financial Ruin: Medical bills can skyrocket in the blink of an eye. Without insurance, you could find yourself drowning in debt, potentially leading to bankruptcy. Even routine check-ups and minor accidents can accumulate hefty bills, leaving you with a crippling financial burden.

Limited Access to Healthcare: Without insurance, your choices of healthcare providers and facilities may be restricted. You might hesitate to seek medical attention when needed, which could lead to delayed treatment and worsened health conditions.

Emergency Expenses: Imagine facing a sudden medical emergency, such as an accident or a severe illness. Without insurance, you'd be solely responsible for all the associated costs, including hospitalization, surgeries, and medication. This can deplete your savings or force you to take on loans with high interest rates or worse, file bankruptcy.

Avoidance of Preventive Care: Routine check-ups and preventive measures are crucial for maintaining good health. Without insurance, you may skip these essential visits due to the fear of expenses. Missing out on preventive care can lead to undiagnosed health issues that could have been addressed early.

Stress and Anxiety: Constant worry about the financial implications of healthcare can take a toll on your mental health. The stress and anxiety of not having a safety net can negatively impact your overall well-being.

No Family Protection: If you have a family, going without health insurance jeopardizes your health and the well-being of your loved ones. An unexpected medical crisis could have a devastating ripple effect on your family's financial stability.

Legal Mandates: Depending on your location, there may be legal requirements to have health insurance. Going without it could result in penalties or fines, adding to your financial burden.

In essence, the absence of health insurance leaves you vulnerable to financial hardship, limited healthcare options, and unnecessary stress. It's not just about the cost of medical care; it's also about your peace of mind and the well-being of you and your family. Health insurance is a vital safety net to protect against the life-threatening consequences of being uninsured.

Choosing Providers and Booking Appointments with Confidence

We'll help you choose a primary care physician and grasp the essentials of scheduling appointments, ensuring you have the knowledge to navigate the healthcare system with confidence.

The objective is to discover a PCP who aligns with your criteria as outlined below.

Check In-Network Providers: Ensure your PCP is in your insurance network to save on costs.

Location Matters: Pick a PCP whose office is easy to reach from your college or home.

Read Reviews: Research PCPs online for feedback on their responsiveness and how they treat patients.

Flexible Hours: Look for a PCP with flexible hours to fit your college schedule.

Telehealth Options: Consider telehealth appointments for convenience and accessibility.

Scheduling: Book appointments online or by phone for your convenience.

Knowing When to Seek Care

Primary Care Physician (PCP):

- ▸ Routine check-ups and preventive care.
- ▸ Non-life-threatening illnesses or conditions.
- ▸ Managing chronic conditions.
- ▸ Prescription refills.
- ▸ Minor injuries or sprains.

▸ Follow-up on ongoing health issues.
▸ Non-severe cold or flu symptoms.
▸ General health concerns or questions.

Urgent Care:

▸ Minor injuries like cuts, burns, or minor fractures.
▸ Mild to moderate allergic reactions.
▸ Fever without severe symptoms.
▸ Sprains and strains.
▸ Minor infections (e.g., ear or sinus infections).
▸ Urinary tract infections (UTIs).
▸ Minor asthma or respiratory issues.
▸ Needed X-rays or lab tests after hours.
▸ Other non-life-threatening but urgent medical needs.

Emergency Room (ER):

▸ Severe injuries, such as head injuries, broken bones, or deep cuts.
▸ Chest pain or severe heart palpitations.
▸ Difficulty breathing or shortness of breath.
▸ Seizures or loss of consciousness.
▸ Severe allergic reactions (e.g., difficulty breathing, swelling of the face).
▸ Signs of a stroke (e.g., sudden weakness, confusion, trouble speaking).
▸ Severe abdominal pain.
▸ High fever with severe symptoms.
▸ Severe burns or electrical injuries.
▸ Severe bleeding or injuries after an accident.
▸ Suicidal thoughts or severe mental health crisis.

Considerations for College Students

Schedule-Friendly: Find healthcare providers who accommodate your busy college life.

Understand Costs: Know your insurance costs, deductibles, and co-payments. Save money by using in-network options.

Digital Accessibility: Explore providers with online appointment booking, telehealth, and medical record access.

Emergency Preparedness: Research nearby hospitals and urgent care centers and keep important medical records handy in emergencies.

So, there you have it—some essential insights to help you navigate the world of healthcare as a young adult. Remember, your health is an investment, and making informed decisions today will pay off in the long run. Don't hesitate to ask questions, explore your options, and stay proactive about your well-being.

Wellness Checks and Preventive Care: Your Health, Your Choice

Taking charge of your health is paramount, especially during the crucial phase of young adulthood. This section will delve into the significance of routine check-ups and preventive care, emphasizing their role in maintaining your well-being. Additionally, we'll provide insights into vaccinations, offering valuable information to empower your healthcare decisions.

The Value of Routine Check-ups

Emphasis on Prevention: Routine check-ups are not just for when you're feeling unwell. They serve as proactive health assessments to identify potential issues before they become major concerns. This approach not only keeps you healthier but can also reduce future healthcare costs.

Integrated Evaluation: Regular check-ups encompass your mental and emotional well-being beyond physical health. This holistic evaluation is particularly important as young adults face the changes and stresses of college or independent living.

Services for Prevention (Screenings, Vaccines, etc.)

A Review of Vaccines: Vaccinations are crucial in preventing various diseases. Staying informed about recommended vaccines is essential for your overall health. College-aged or not, vaccines protect you and the community.

Assessing Potential: Early screenings, such as those for STIs, high blood pressure, and cholesterol, are like health checkpoints. These screenings are tailored to your age and risk factors, identifying and addressing potential health problems promptly.

Primary Care Physician's Recommended Visit Frequency:

Notes on Particulars: Depending on your unique health situation, lifestyle, or mental health needs, you may require more frequent check-ups. Collaborate with your PCP to establish a suitable visit plan that aligns with your health goals.

Things to Bring to Your Doctor's Appointments and What to Ask

Addressing Health Issues: Open communication between you and your healthcare professional is key to understanding your condition fully. Preparing questions and providing detailed, honest information about your symptoms and lifestyle empowers your healthcare provider to make the best decisions for your health.

Making Sense of Treatment Programs: Treatment plans are more effective when you clearly understand them. Ask your healthcare provider about the reasoning behind treatment suggestions, potential side effects, and how to integrate these recommendations into your daily life, whether you're a college student or living independently.

Check for Mental Health: Your mental health directly impacts your physical well-being. Regardless of your age or living situation, be open and honest about any stress, difficulties, or mental health issues you're facing. Your PCP can provide support, referrals, or services if needed.

Vaccinations and Immunizations

Comprehending the Timetable for Vaccines: Staying updated on recommended vaccines, including booster shots if necessary, ensures the best protection against preventable diseases. Your vaccination needs can evolve as you transition from adolescence to adulthood.

Vaccinations Tailored to Your Needs: Some vaccines, like those for meningitis, are particularly important for young adults, especially if you're in college or living in shared housing. Discuss with your doctor before such transitions.

Common Vaccines for Young Adults: Besides standard vaccinations, young adults should consider getting the annual flu shot to protect themselves and those around them. The HPV vaccine is vital for cancer prevention, and vaccines like meningitis and Tdap are essential for maintaining good health.

Vaccination Locations

Healthcare on Campus: Many colleges offer vaccination services on campus, making it convenient for students. Check with your college's health services for information on available vaccines.

Primary Care Physician (PCP): Your PCP can offer tailored recommendations and administer them in the office, taking into account your medical history and current health condition.

Pharmacy and Health Centers: Vaccines are available at many local clinics and pharmacies. If you're a young adult living independently, inquire about vaccination services at your neighborhood pharmacy or health center.

Managing Prescriptions and Medications

Taking control of your health means understanding how to manage prescriptions and medications effectively. This knowledge is valuable for individuals of all ages. It's essential to be informed about your medications, their potential effects on your health, and how to use them responsibly. This proactive approach empowers you to make sound decisions and take charge of your well-being. Whether you have a chronic condition or require occasional treatments, responsible medication management is a crucial aspect of maintaining good health.

Understanding Your Medication

Purpose and Dosage: Knowing why you're taking a particular medication and the correct dosage is essential. Ask your healthcare provider about its function and the recommended dose.

Potential Side Effects: Don't hesitate to consult with your pharmacist about your medications, including potential side effects and what to do if they occur.

Managing Medication Dispensing

Choosing a Pharmacy: Convenience matters when it comes to refilling your prescriptions. Select a pharmacy with convenient hours and, if available, prescription delivery services.

Insurance Information: To minimize out-of-pocket costs, provide your insurance details when filling prescriptions. Familiarize yourself with co-payments and any additional expenses.

Utilizing Copay Cards: Ask your provider about copay cards that can help to reduce the cost of your prescription

GoodRx: GoodRx is a handy app and website that helps you find the best prices for your prescription medications. It provides a list of nearby pharmacies, along with the prices they charge, and offers access to discounts and coupons that can significantly lower your out-of-pocket costs. Whether you have insurance or not, GoodRx can be a valuable tool in reducing the financial burden of healthcare expenses."

Considering Generic Options: Generic medications are often more affordable and equally effective as brand-name ones. Discuss generic alternatives with your healthcare provider or pharmacist.

Tracking Prescription Refills: Don't forget when your prescriptions need refilling. Setting up automatic refills or using reminders can help you stay on track.

Ensuring Proper Medication Adherence

Follow Prescribed Instructions: The key to successful medication outcomes lies in strict adherence to your prescribed regimen. Always follow your healthcare provider's instructions regarding timing and dosage meticulously. If you ever have any uncertainties, don't hesitate to seek guidance from your healthcare professional. For instance, if you're prescribed a 10-day course of antibiotics, completing the full duration is crucial to effectively treating the underlying condition.

Safe Storage: Proper storage is crucial for maintaining medication effectiveness and safety. Always check the expiration date and store medications as directed (e.g., in a cool, dry place). Ensure the safety of your medications, especially when there are pets or young children in your environment, as their accidental access can lead to severe consequences.

Inform Your Healthcare Providers: Keeping your healthcare providers informed about changes in your health, new symptoms, or medication changes is essential for effective treatment. Immediately notify your doctor of any changes.

Addressing Potential Interactions: It's essential to grasp the potential for drug interactions to prevent any undesirable consequences. Have an open conversation with your healthcare provider or pharmacist about any worries regarding drug interactions. You can also utilize reliable websites like Drugs. com to evaluate potential drug interactions and make informed decisions about your medications.

Be Prepared: Unforeseen circumstances can occur, such as missed doses or adverse reactions. Create a plan for dealing with such situations or seek medical help when in doubt.

Understanding prescription drugs, the prescription-filling process, and medication safety procedures is essential for young adults, whether they're in college or not. Active participation in medication management ensures effective treatment and proactive health maintenance.

Estimates and Payment Options

Whether you're planning for dental, vision, or medical procedures, it's crucial to have a clear understanding of the associated costs. Taking this proactive approach helps you prepare financially and make well-informed decisions about your healthcare. It prevents unexpected bills, allows you to explore suitable payment plans, and ensures you maximize your insurance benefits. By taking these steps in advance, you can reduce stress and confidently manage the financial aspects of your healthcare.

Request Estimates: Ask your healthcare provider for a detailed estimate of the proposed treatment, including all associated costs.

Payment Plans: Many healthcare facilities offer flexible payment options, allowing you to spread the cost of treatment over several months.

Financing: Inquire about financing options to help cover the expenses of procedures, especially for more costly treatments.

Charity Care and Federal Poverty Discounts: Additionally, some healthcare institutions offer charity care programs and federal poverty discounts for individuals or families who meet specific income criteria. These programs can provide significant financial relief, so don't hesitate to inquire about them if needed.

Understanding your insurance coverage, exploring coverage options, reviewing benefits for various procedures, and obtaining estimates for healthcare services while considering payment plans and financing can empower you to make informed decisions about your health and effectively manage the financial aspects of your care.

Dental Health and Oral Care

As you step into adulthood, prioritizing your oral health becomes paramount. It goes beyond having a captivating smile; it profoundly influences your overall well-being. In this section, we will embark on a journey to explore the vital facets of dental health and oral care, equipping you with the wisdom and practices necessary for a lifetime filled with healthy smiles and optimal health. Remember those lessons from childhood about regular teeth brushing, flossing, and those routine dentist visits? Now, let's uncover why these practices are indispensable for your oral health as you navigate the path to adulthood.

The Value of Good Oral Hygiene

Preventive Characteristics: Maintaining good oral health is your first defense against issues like cavities and gum disease. Regular oral care practices are key to preserving the health and longevity of your teeth and gums.

The Importance of Oral Health to Total Health: Oral health is intricately connected to your overall well-being. Neglecting oral hygiene can have far-reaching consequences, potentially contributing to broader health problems. A healthy mouth is a cornerstone of good health in general.

Locating a Dentist and Making Appointments for Dental Treatment

Access to Dental Services: Ensuring easy access to dental care is essential. Whether in an urban or rural area, finding a local dentist and establishing a consistent dental care routine guarantees that your oral health needs are met.

Making Regular Appointments: Consistency is key when it comes to oral health. Regular dental check-ups are preventive measures that help detect and address oral health issues early, allowing for timely intervention and treatment. Most insurances cover a dental cleaning 2x per year.

Dental Plans and Their Coverage

Dental insurance and coverage options are essential considerations when it comes to managing the costs of dental care. Here's what you need to know:

Dental Insurance: Dental insurance can provide financial assistance for routine and emergency dental care. To make the most of your coverage, familiarize yourself with your policy, including:

- **Covered Services:** Know which dental services are covered by your insurance, such as preventive care, basic procedures, and major treatments.

- **Benefits Breakdown:** Pay attention to the details of your benefits, especially for common procedures like cavity repair, root canals, braces, and more. Understand what percentage of the cost is covered by your insurance.

Coverage Options: In addition to individual dental insurance plans, consider other options:

- **Health Plans:** Some health insurance plans include dental coverage as an add-on or part of a comprehensive package.
- **Employer-Sponsored Plans:** If employed, your employer may offer dental insurance as part of your benefits package.
- **Supplemental Dental Plans:** These plans can complement your existing coverage or fill gaps in dental care.

Helpful Hints for Keeping Your Teeth Clean

Effective Oral Hygiene Practices: Consistently brushing and flossing teeth is the cornerstone of good oral hygiene. These simple habits prevent plaque buildup, support healthy gums, and reduce the risk of cavities. For best results, brush 2x per day, and floss at least once per day.

Mindful Diet Choices: Be conscious of your diet, particularly sugary foods and beverages. Reducing sugar intake can significantly lower the risk of tooth decay and oral health problems.

Emphasizing Fluoride: Fluoride is essential for strengthening tooth enamel and preventing cavities. Incorporate fluoride toothpaste into your daily oral care routine and consider fluoride treatments if your dentist recommends.

Oral Safety During Physical Activities: Protecting your teeth during sports and physical activities is crucial. Wearing a mouthguard can prevent dental injuries, preserving your oral health.

Avoiding Harmful Habits: Limiting alcohol consumption and abstaining from smoking are essential for oral health. These habits can worsen oral health problems and negatively impact your overall well-being.

Your oral health is a vital component of your overall health. By understanding the importance of dental health, finding a local dentist, navigating dental insurance, and practicing effective oral hygiene, you'll be well-equipped to ensure a lifetime of healthy smiles and optimal well-being.

Clear Vision: Nurturing Your Eye Health

Clear vision is a window to the world and a vital component of your overall well-being, especially as a young adult. In this section, we'll delve into the importance of eye care, focusing on annual eye exams and vision-related considerations that can impact your academic and personal life. Let's explore how prioritizing your eye health can pave the way for a future filled with clear vision and optimal performance.

Why It's Crucial to Have Annual Eye Exams

Preventive: Regular eye exams play a crucial role in preventive care, helping to identify potential issues before they escalate into major concerns. Make it a priority to schedule these check-ups to keep a close watch on your eye health. Typical exams are done at least annually.

Academic & Career Impact: Maintaining optimal vision is not merely a matter of eye health; it profoundly influences academic excellence and professional accomplishments. Impaired eyesight can hinder your academic performance by affecting your reading, writing, and learning ability. Moreover, in the professional sphere, vision problems may undermine your career by impeding your performance, limiting job opportunities, and affecting your overall success. Whether you're a student striving for academic excellence or a professional aiming to advance in your career, the importance of clear vision cannot be underestimated.

Safe Driving: Annual vision exams are essential for maintaining good eyesight and play a crucial role in safe driving. These regular check-ups help detect changes in your vision that could affect your ability to drive safely, such as refractive errors or eye conditions. By addressing vision issues promptly through annual exams, you can ensure that you have a clear and accurate vision on the road, contributing to safer driving experiences for yourself and others.

Seeking the Services of an Eye Doctor

Local Eye Care Professionals: Building a relationship with a nearby optometrist or ophthalmologist guarantees ongoing and accessible eye care. Young adults, inquire about vision care options in your neighborhood. When in doubt, seek recommendations from others.

Why You Should Get Your Eyes Examined Regularly

Optimal Vision and Early Detection: Regular eye exams offer two invaluable benefits – maintaining optimal vision and detecting potential problems early. Follow your eye doctor's advice and schedule regular check-ups every year or as recommended.

Understanding Vision Insurance and Maximizing Benefits

Navigating vision insurance is crucial to effectively manage the costs of eye care. Here are some valuable tips to consider:

Vision Insurance Overview: Vision insurance typically covers some of the costs associated with eye care, including eye exams, eyeglasses, and contact lenses. However, the specifics of coverage can vary from one plan to another.

Know Your Plan: Review your vision insurance policy carefully. Pay attention to:

- **Coverage Limits:** Some vision insurance plans restrict how often they cover certain services. For example, they may only provide coverage for a new pair of eyeglasses or contact lenses every other year.
- **Dollar Amounts:** Many plans have a maximum amount they'll pay for eyeglasses or contact lenses. Anything beyond this limit becomes your responsibility.
- **In-Network Providers:** Find out which eye doctors and optical centers are in-network. Visiting in-network providers often results in lower out-of-pocket expenses.

- ▸ **Estimate Costs:** Before committing to vision care services, request your eye care provider's estimates. This can help you understand the potential out-of-pocket expenses and make informed decisions.
- ▸ **Compare Options:** If your insurance plan covers eyeglasses and contact lenses, compare the costs and benefits of each option. Some plans may provide more generous coverage for one type of corrective eyewear.
- ▸ **Utilize Flexible Spending Accounts (FSAs) or Health Savings Accounts (HSAs):** If you have an FSA or HSA, consider using these tax-advantaged accounts to pay for vision-related expenses not covered by insurance.

Prescription Updates: If your prescription changes, update your eyeglasses or contact lenses accordingly. Wearing the correct prescription helps maintain clear vision and prevents eye strain.

Inquire About Discounts: Some vision insurance plans offer discounts on additional services, such as laser eye surgery or designer eyewear frames. Don't hesitate to ask your provider about available discounts.

By knowing the specifics of your vision insurance plan, estimating costs before committing to eye care services, and maximizing your benefits, you can effectively manage your eye health while optimizing your insurance coverage.

Mastering Eyewear Choices and Responsible Usage

Eyeglass Frames: When selecting eyeglass frames, consider factors like comfort, style, and how they complement your face shape and lifestyle. As a young adult, your frames should reflect your style and cater to your active life.

Proper Care of Contact Lenses: Maintaining clean and infection-free contact lenses is essential for preserving good vision. Always use the prescribed cleaning solution and practice thorough handwashing before handling lenses.

Using eyewear Responsibly: Responsible eyewear use is vital. Avoid leaving contacts in for extended periods, as it can lead to issues like ulcers. Use your glasses when required and follow your eye doctor's recommendations.

Preventing Eye Strain: Extended screen time can lead to eye strain. Remember the 20-20-20 rule – take a 20-second break every 20 minutes and focus on something 20 feet away to alleviate eye strain caused by screen use.

Prioritizing your eye health through regular exams, finding a local eye care professional, understanding vision insurance, practicing proper eyeglasses and contact lens care, and using your eyewear responsibly are essential steps to ensure clear vision and peak performance in your academic and personal pursuits.

Key Takeaways

Understanding Health Insurance

- When choosing health insurance, carefully evaluate costs, coverage, and provider networks based on your healthcare needs.
- Consider potential out-of-pocket expenses, including deductibles and co-pays.
- Ensure your preferred healthcare providers are in-network, and assess coverage for specific health needs.

The Significance of Health Insurance

- Health insurance serves as a financial safety net, covering unexpected medical expenses.
- Going without health insurance can lead to financial ruin, limited healthcare access, and avoidance of preventive care.
- It provides peace of mind and safeguards your family's financial stability.

Wellness Checks and Preventive Care

- Routine check-ups are essential for proactive health assessments.
- Early screenings, vaccinations, and regular visits to a primary care physician help maintain good health.

‣ Effective communication with healthcare providers is crucial for understanding your health condition and treatment plans.

Clear Vision and Eye Health

‣ Annual eye exams are vital for maintaining optimal vision and preventing vision-related issues.
‣ Good eye health positively impacts academic and career success and safe driving.
‣ Understand your vision insurance coverage, seek services from local eye care professionals, and make responsible eyewear choices.

Test Your Knowledge

1. Why is it important to have health insurance if you can?
   a. To avoid taxes
   b. To get discounts on gym memberships
   c. To protect yourself from high medical costs
   d. To receive free healthcare
2. Why are wellness visits and preventive care important?
   a. They help you avoid going to the gym
   b. They ensure you get sick often
   c. They detect and prevent health issues early
   d. They provide opportunities to eat more junk food
3. How can getting an estimate of cost help you?
   a. It enables you to win a bet with your friends
   b. It allows you to plan your budget and make informed decisions
   c. It enables you to avoid medical appointments altogether
   d. It guarantees you the lowest price for any medical service
4. How can you help keep your oral care healthy?
   a. By brushing and flossing regularly and scheduling dental check-ups.
   b. By eating a balanced diet and limiting sugary snacks.
   c. By avoiding tobacco and excessive alcohol consumption.

      d.   All of the above.

5.   What is the difference between in and out-of-network?

      a.   In-network providers offer better and cheaper services

      b.   In-network is for weekdays, out-of-network is for weekends

      c.   In-network providers have agreements with your insurance company, while out-of-network providers do not

      d.   In-network providers are located indoors, while out-of-network providers are located outdoors

6.   A fixed amount you pay for a service is called what?

      a.   Co-insurance

      b.   Out-of-pocket

      c.   Premium

      d.   Co-pay

CHAPTER 2

Relationships and Sexual Health

L et me introduce you to Alex - a young adult who found themselves in a bit of a pickle because they didn't have the right info about relationships and sexual health.

So, picture this: Alex started seeing someone they really liked, and things got pretty serious. They wanted to take their relationship to the next level but didn't know how to have an open and honest conversation about it. They felt kinda awkward bringing up the topic of consent and protection because, well, they'd never really talked about it with anyone.

Long story short, Alex and their partner ended up in a situation where lines got blurred, and they didn't discuss their boundaries or use protection. Unfortunately, this resulted in Alex contracting a sexually transmitted infection (STI). It was a bit of a mess, and it left Alex feeling confused and worried about their health.

Alex had to take the responsible step of seeking medical treatment. They made an appointment with a healthcare provider, and during that visit, they had to have an open and honest conversation about what had happened. It was a bit uncomfortable, but it was crucial for their health and well-being.

Now, Alex faces the challenge of discussing this information with any potential new partners in the future, emphasizing the importance of clear communication, consent, and protection in intimate relationships.

Now, here's the kicker - all this could have been avoided with some knowledge about consent, protection, and open communication. That's exactly what this chapter is here for - to make sure you don't have to learn things the hard way like Alex did. We're going to equip you with the tools and know-how to handle these situations confidently and responsibly. So, let's dive in and make sure you're prepared for whatever comes your way!

How to Be Safe on Dates

Ensuring Your Safety During Dates

Dating can be an exciting and enjoyable experience, but it's essential to prioritize safety for everyone, regardless of gender. Whether meeting someone for the first time or going on subsequent dates, taking precautionary measures ensures a secure and enjoyable dating experience. Here are key strategies on how to stay safe during your dates:

Personal Safety Precautions

Trust Your Instincts: Always listen to your gut feelings. If something feels off or uncomfortable during a date, prioritize your safety. Trusting your intuition can help you make quick decisions to protect yourself.

Limit Personal Information: As you're getting to know someone, it's important to strike a balance between sharing and safeguarding your personal information. It's a good idea to hold back on sharing things like your home address, financial details, or sensitive personal history in the early stages of the relationship. Instead, focus on building trust and gradually sharing these aspects of your life as your relationship deepens and you feel more comfortable doing so.

Be Mindful of Alcohol Consumption: If you consume alcohol during your date, do so responsibly. Watch your drink at all times; never leave it unattended. Know your limits and avoid excessive drinking. Being in control of your faculties is crucial for personal safety.

Communicating Your Plans

Inform Someone You Trust:

1. Before going on a date, inform a trusted friend or family member about your plans.
2. Share details such as the location, time, and who you'll be meeting.

3. Provide periodic updates if plans change or if you decide to go to a different location.

Establish a Check-In System: Set up a check-in system with a friend during the date. This could involve sending a quick text at a predetermined time to confirm that you're okay. If your date extends into the evening, periodic check-ins can provide peace of mind.

Emergency Code Word: Create a word or phrase with a friend. If you feel uncomfortable or need assistance during the date, you can discreetly use this code to signal that you need help. This code can be useful for communicating distress without alarming your date.

Meeting in Public Places

Choose Public Venues: Opt for public places for the first few dates. Coffee shops, restaurants, or public parks provide a safer environment with other people around. Public venues also offer an easy exit if you need to leave the date quickly.

Daytime Meetings: Consider daytime meetings for initial encounters. Daylight hours generally offer increased visibility and a more secure atmosphere. It's easier to assess your date's character in well-lit settings.

Avoid Private Residences Initially: Refrain from visiting private residences or inviting someone to your home during the early stages of dating. Getting to know each other in public settings is safer, where you can gauge compatibility without compromising your safety.

Sharing Location Details

Share Live Location: Use location-sharing features on your smartphone with a trusted friend. Many messaging apps offer this option, allowing someone to track your live location during the date. Sharing your location can be reassuring for both you and your loved ones.

Emergency Services App: Consider using safety apps designed for emergencies. These apps often include features like panic buttons and location tracking. Quick access to emergency services or designated contacts can provide an extra layer of security.

Stay Connected: Keep your phone charged and stay connected throughout the date. Ensure you have a means of communication in case you need assistance or need to make an emergency call. A charged phone can be a lifeline in unexpected situations.

Dating should be an enjoyable and positive experience; these safety precautions are intended to help ensure it remains so. By prioritizing personal safety, communicating your plans, meeting in public places, and sharing location details, you contribute to a safer dating environment for yourself and others.

Online Dating Safety Tips for Young Adults

Online dating has become a common way for people to meet and connect. While it provides exciting opportunities, prioritizing safety and informed choices is crucial. Here are essential tips to navigate online dating securely:

Creating a Secure Online Profile

Your online dating profile is your digital introduction, and creating a secure profile is the first step in establishing a positive online presence while safeguarding your privacy.

Here's how to do it:

Limit Personal Information: Avoid sharing sensitive details in your profile, such as home address, phone number, or financial information. These should be reserved for private conversations once trust has been established.

Unique Photos: Use unique and recent photos for your profile. Avoid using images that can be reverse-searched to find your identity. This helps protect your privacy and ensures authenticity.

Mindful Username: Choose a username that doesn't reveal too much personal information. Avoid using your full name or anything easily associated with your offline identity.

Privacy Settings: Familiarize yourself with the privacy settings of the dating platform. Adjust settings to control who can view your profile and contact you. This step allows you to manage your online visibility effectively.

Safety Precautions for Online Interactions

Engaging in online conversations requires safety precautions to create a secure and positive environment.

Messaging within the App: Keep initial communications within the dating app's messaging system. Avoid sharing personal contact information until you've established a level of trust. This adds a layer of security.

Beware of Red Flags: Be vigilant for red flags such as requests for money, overly aggressive behavior, or inconsistencies in the information provided. Report any suspicious activity to the platform administrators.

Avoid Clicking on Suspicious Links: Be cautious about clicking on links shared by someone you've just met online. These links could lead to phishing sites or malware. Verify the legitimacy of any links before clicking.

Report Inappropriate Behavior: Most dating platforms have reporting features. If you encounter inappropriate behavior or harassment, promptly report it to the platform administrators. This helps maintain a safe community.

Online Photo Safety: Online safety is paramount, so it's crucial to remember not to send photos of yourself, especially anything you wouldn't want others to see. Once an image is shared online, it can be challenging to control where it ends up, so always exercise caution and think twice before hitting that send button.

Meeting Online Contacts Offline

▸ When meeting online contacts offline, remember to prioritize safety and refer back to the 'How to Be Safe on Dates' section for valuable tips and precautions.

Cultivating Healthy and Fulfilling Romantic Relationships

Your transition into young adulthood opens up a world of opportunities, including exploring the intricacies of romantic relationships. Building these connections involves effective communication, self-awareness, conflict

RELATIONSHIPS AND SEXUAL HEALTH

resolution skills, and setting clear boundaries and expectations. Here's a comprehensive guide to help you navigate the path of healthy romance:

Effective Communication in Relationships

Open and Honest Dialogue: Create an environment where you and your partner feel safe expressing your thoughts and feelings without judgment. Open communication is the foundation of a strong bond. To truly understand your partner's perspective, practice active listening. Take a moment to reflect on their words before responding – it's a powerful way to nurture mutual understanding.

Expressing Needs and Desires: Clear communication of your needs, desires, and expectations can prevent misunderstandings and lay the groundwork for trust within your relationship.

Non-Verbal Communication: Pay attention to non-verbal cues like body language, such as maintaining eye contact, and facial expressions like smiles and laughter; sometimes, they convey more than words ever could.

Respectful Disagreement: Disagreements are part of any relationship, but it's vital to handle them respectfully. Avoid personal attacks and focus on the issue at hand – this fosters a healthier conflict resolution process.

Recognizing Red Flags and Warning Signs

Lack of Respect: Watch for signs of disrespect, such as belittling comments or dismissive behavior. A healthy relationship thrives on mutual respect and appreciation. It's important to value and uplift each other, recognizing the worth and feelings of both partners.

Controlling Behavior: Be cautious of controlling tendencies. Healthy relationships are based on autonomy and mutual decision-making rather than one person exerting dominance. Remember that both individuals should have equal say and influence in the relationship.

Isolation: It may raise concerns if your partner isolates you from friends and family. Healthy relationships encourage social connections and

38 | LIFE SKILLS 101

personal growth. Being supportive of each other's social lives and personal development is a sign of a strong partnership.

Unwillingness to Compromise: Inflexibility and an unwillingness to compromise can indicate potential issues. Successful relationships involve give-and-take to meet each other's needs. Flexibility and compromise are key ingredients for a harmonious relationship.

Consistent Dishonesty: Trust is the foundation of any healthy relationship, and consistent dishonesty can erode it. Be attentive to any signs of deception. Building trust through honesty and transparency is essential for a strong and lasting bond.

Conflict Resolution Strategies

Stay Calm: Emotions can run high during conflicts but strive to keep them in check. Communicating calmly helps prevent tensions from escalating. Maintaining a level head can lead to more productive discussions.

Focus on the Issue: Address the issue causing conflict rather than bringing up unrelated grievances. This approach maintains clarity and relevance, making it easier to find solutions to specific problems.

Seek Compromise: Aim for compromise. Finding a middle ground allows both partners to feel heard and respected. Compromise is a key aspect of healthy conflict resolution.

Take Breaks When Needed: If emotions become overwhelming, taking breaks can provide clarity and perspective before revisiting the discussion. Sometimes stepping away briefly can help you come back to the issue with a fresh perspective.

Learn from Conflicts: View conflicts as opportunities for growth. Understanding each other's perspectives and learning from disagreements strengthens the relationship. Conflict can be a catalyst for positive change and greater understanding.

By mastering these effective communication techniques, spotting potential warning signs, and using conflict resolution strategies, you'll find yourself navigating the intricate world of romantic relationships with confidence.

Setting clear boundaries and expectations is key, helping you focus on healthy, respectful, and growth-oriented connections. It's all part of your journey towards meaningful and fulfilling relationships.

Understanding Sexual Health

Alright, folks, it's time to switch gears and dive into a topic that might make some of you blush, but hey, it's a part of growing up, right? We're talking about sexual health – a crucial aspect of your well-being as you navigate the maze of young adulthood. This chapter isn't about awkward lectures or shying away from the subject. It's about giving you the knowledge and tools to make informed choices and ensure a healthy, respectful, and enjoyable journey in this aspect of your life. So, brace yourselves for some important, honest, and open conversations as we explore the ins and outs of sexual health.

Responsible and Safe Sexual Practices

Engaging in responsible sexual practices is a fundamental aspect of maintaining the well-being of both partners.

Here are key considerations for a healthy and safe approach to intimacy:

Using Protection: Using protection, such as condoms and other contraception methods, plays a crucial role in keeping both partners safe from STIs and unplanned pregnancies. It's a shared responsibility that ensures the well-being of everyone involved.

Talking About Protection: Open and honest communication with your partner about contraception is essential. It's about making sure you're both on the same page when it comes to your sexual health. Discussing preferences and choices is a vital part of the conversation.

Getting Tested: Regular STI tests are a smart move, especially if you're in a non-monogamous relationship. These tests help catch any potential issues early, allowing for prompt treatment and preventing the spread of infections.

Knowing Each Other's Status: Honesty about your STI status and being informed about your partner's status is crucial. It's a way to build trust and maintain safe practices in your relationship, ensuring everyone's well-being.

Trying Other Things: Exploring non-penetrative sexual activities can be a fun and safe way to enjoy intimacy. Before trying anything new, have an open and respectful discussion with your partner to establish boundaries and preferences.

Taking Care of Your Reproductive Health: Regular check-ups with your healthcare provider cover various aspects of reproductive health. These check-ups address everything from contraception options to discussions about fertility.

Checking Your Contraception: If you're using hormonal contraception, remember to schedule regular check-ups to ensure it remains the right choice for you and is effective in meeting your needs.

Mental Well-being Matters: Your mental health is connected to your sexual well-being. During check-ups, don't hesitate to discuss any concerns related to your sexual experiences or relationships, as it's essential for your overall well-being.

Understanding Consent

Consent is a mutual and voluntary agreement among all parties involved in a sexual activity. It must be clear, enthusiastic, and can be changed or withdrawn at any time. So, always make sure all individuals involved are on the same page and comfortable with what's happening.

Key Points on Consent:

Communication is Key: Understanding consent requires open communication between sexual partners. Discussing boundaries, desires, and expectations before engaging in any sexual activity is fundamental for a consensual and respectful experience.

Freely Given: Consent must be given freely without coercion, manipulation, or pressure. It should never be assumed or obtained through force or intimidation. Everyone involved should feel entirely comfortable with the decisions being made.

Capacity to Consent: Individuals must possess the capacity to consent, meaning they are of legal age, mentally competent, and not under the influence of substances that impair judgment. Consent is not valid if any of the parties cannot give it.

Revocable: Consent can be revoked at any point during the sexual activity. The activity should cease immediately if someone expresses discomfort or changes their mind. Respecting boundaries is essential for a healthy experience.

As you embrace sexual health education, tap into the resources available to you, and make safe practices a part of your lives, you'll be well-equipped to confidently navigate the intricate world of intimate relationships. Your focus on well-being, respect for one another, and your journey of growth isn't just for your younger years – it's a foundation for a fulfilling future.

Key Takeaways

Prioritize Personal Safety in Dating: When dating, always prioritize personal safety. Trust your instincts, limit initial personal information sharing, and communicate your plans with someone you trust. Taking precautions ensures a secure and enjoyable dating experience.

Online Dating Safety: For those exploring online dating, create a secure online profile by limiting personal information, using unique photos, and familiarizing yourself with privacy settings. Practice safe online interactions and meet online contacts in public places initially.

Understand Sexual Health: Comprehensive sexual education is crucial for making informed decisions about sexual health, including contraception, consent, and responsible practices. It fosters respect and inclusivity and reduces the stigma surrounding sexual health topics.

Healthy Romantic Relationships: Cultivate healthy and fulfilling romantic relationships through effective communication, recognizing warning signs, employing conflict resolution strategies, and setting clear boundaries and expectations. Prioritize emotional safety, trust, and mutual growth.

Test Your Knowledge

1. What is an essential aspect of cultivating healthy romantic relationships?
   a. Avoiding communication
   b. Being secretive about your feelings
   c. Open and honest communication
   d. Ignoring each other's needs

2. Why is it crucial to practice safe dating on dates?
   a. To impress your date
   b. To maintain a sense of mystery
   c. To ensure your safety
   d. To make the date more exciting

3. What is an integral part of understanding sexual health?
   a. Practicing safe sex
   b. Regular health check-ups
   c. Being informed about contraceptives
   d. All of the above

4. Which of the following is an example of an unhealthy romantic relationship?
   a. Open communication and mutual respect
   b. Regular conflict resolution
   c. Emotional abuse and control
   d. Shared responsibilities

5. What does consent mean in the context of sexual activity?
   a. It means agreeing to engage in sexual activity without any prior communication.
   b. It implies that only verbal consent is required.
   c. It signifies the voluntary, clear, and enthusiastic agreement by all parties involved.
   d. It encompasses clear communication, mutual agreement, and willingness from all parties involved.

CHAPTER 3

Social Etiquette

In our fast-paced world, social interactions shape our daily lives. Think about the time you walked into your significant other's home to meet their parents for the first time, filled with excitement and nervousness, or the moments spent mingling at a family gathering, hoping to make a positive impression. Imagine engaging in online conversations, where words can have a lasting impact.

Now, let me share a story with you. Meet Brandon, a teenager getting ready to meet their partner's family for the first time. Brandon was eager to make a great impression, but he underestimated the importance of social etiquette. During dinner, Brandon started talking loudly about a topic that made some family members uncomfortable, and because Brandon was not watching for other's reactions or noticing that they were not engaging, this led to awkward silences and a less-than-pleasant atmosphere.

Now, imagine if Brandon had known the art of social etiquette. They would have been mindful of the conversation topics, listened actively to what others had to say, and used their manners at the dinner table. The interaction would have been smoother, and Brandon would have left a positive impression on their partner's family.

In various scenarios, understanding the nuances of social etiquette isn't just a skill; it's your secret weapon. It's the key that unlocks doors to success, be it in your personal relationships, social gatherings, or the digital realm.

This chapter on social etiquette is more than just a guide; it's your practical toolkit for navigating the world of social interactions. It offers tips and insights to help you present yourself confidently, treat others respectfully, and create meaningful connections in various social settings. With practical advice that's easy to follow and culturally sensitive, this chapter empowers you to navigate the social landscape with grace and courtesy, ensuring your interactions are not just pleasant but also profoundly impactful.

Introduction to Social Etiquette

In the complex world of social interactions, knowing your way around social etiquette is like having a superpower. It can make a huge difference in how people see you, the connections you make, and how your interactions play out. This chapter is your guide to mastering social etiquette, specifically tailored for teens and young adults. We'll dive into why it matters and how it can supercharge your social life.

Understanding the Significance of Social Etiquette

Social etiquette is the compass that guides us through the labyrinth of social interactions. It encompasses the unwritten rules that govern behavior, communication, and courtesy in various social settings. For young adults stepping into adulthood, grasping the importance of social etiquette is paramount. It transcends mere politeness; it manifests respect, consideration, and cultural awareness in our diverse and dynamic world.

By adhering to social etiquette, individuals signal their understanding of societal norms, radiating sophistication and awareness that leads to positive impressions. Recognizing the significance of social etiquette lays the foundation for successful interactions, whether in professional arenas, social gatherings, or personal relationships. It paves the way for meaningful connections and underscores an individual's commitment to gracefully navigating the intricate tapestry of social spaces.

How Proper Etiquette Enhances Your Social Interactions

Proper etiquette is the oil that lubricates the gears of social engagement, ensuring smoother and more positive interactions. It elevates the quality of relationships and contributes to a harmonious and respectful social environment. Here's how proper etiquette enhances our social interactions:

- **First Impressions**: As the saying goes, first impressions are lasting impressions. Exhibiting proper etiquette from the outset leaves a lasting, favorable mark on others. Whether in a job interview, meeting new acquaintances, or attending social functions, a well-mannered demeanor establishes a positive bedrock for future interactions.

- **Building Trust and Respect:** Etiquette is the cornerstone of trust and respect among individuals. Respectful behavior, active listening, and consideration for others' feelings create an atmosphere of trust. This is particularly pivotal in professional settings, where trust is integral to collaboration and success.

- **Cultural Sensitivity:** Social etiquette extends to cultural sensitivity. Recognizing and respecting cultural differences in greetings, gestures, and communication styles demonstrates global awareness and receptiveness to diverse perspectives. This, in turn, fosters inclusivity in social interactions.

- **Effective Communication:** Etiquette plays a pivotal role in effective communication. It guides individuals in expressing themselves respectfully, resolving conflicts diplomatically, and engaging in conversations without causing discomfort. Effective communication stands as the bedrock of successful social interactions.

- **Professional Advancement:** In the professional world, adherence to proper etiquette is a stepping stone to career advancement. Whether at networking events, business meetings, or workplace interactions, individuals with polished social skills are more likely to be considered for opportunities and promotions.

- **Positive Atmosphere in Social Spaces:** Proper etiquette contributes to a positive and comfortable atmosphere in social spaces. Whether attending formal events or casual gatherings, individuals who observe social norms create an environment where everyone feels valued and at ease.

Now that you're all set to boost your social skills, let's dive into various social situations and learn how to handle them with confidence and grace.

Mastering Group Social Events

Inviting Friends or Colleagues to Social Events

Effective Communication: When inviting friends or colleagues to social events, clear communication is key. Providing essential event details, such as the date, time, venue, and any special instructions, helps your guests plan their schedules and ensures everyone is on the same page. Make RSVPing easy, whether it's through a text message or a digital invitation that allows a simple click to RSVP.

Consideration for Preferences: Extend invitations thoughtfully by considering the preferences and availability of those you invite. Opt for event times and types that accommodate diverse interests and commitments. This approach increases the likelihood of a successful and enjoyable gathering.

Inclusive Invitations: Prioritize inclusivity when extending invitations. Avoid language or behaviors that might inadvertently make others feel excluded. Creating a welcoming and comfortable environment for all attendees enhances the overall experience.

RSVP Etiquette: When sending out invitations, it's a good practice to request RSVPs from your invitees. This not only helps with event planning but also ensures that everyone can anticipate and enjoy the gathering without any logistical surprises.

Choosing the Right Venue for Gatherings

Consider Group Size: Select venues based on the size of your group, ensuring that the chosen location can comfortably accommodate all attendees. Overcrowded spaces can hinder social interactions, so be mindful of the number of guests.

Variety of Venues: Diversify your venue choices based on the nature of the gathering. Opt for settings that align with the occasion, whether it's a casual coffee shop for a low-key meet-up, a vibrant restaurant for a birthday celebration, or a formal venue for a special event. Adapting the venue to the occasion enhances the overall experience.

Accessibility: Factor in the venue's accessibility, location, transportation options, and any special needs of your guests. Ensure that everyone can easily reach the location, taking into consideration factors like proximity to public transport and parking availability.

Ambiance and Atmosphere: Pay attention to the ambiance and atmosphere of the chosen venue. The setting should complement the mood of the event, such as a cozy cafe for a relaxed gathering or a more upscale restaurant for formal occasions. The right ambiance enhances the overall enjoyment of the gathering.

Dressing Appropriately for Different Occasions

Understand the Dress Code: Familiarize yourself with the event's dress code, whether it's casual, business casual, or formal attire. Dressing appropriately demonstrates respect for the occasion and consideration for fellow attendees, ensuring you blend seamlessly into the social setting.

Grooming and Personal Hygiene: Prioritize grooming and personal hygiene when preparing for social events. A well-groomed appearance leaves a positive impression and shows that you value your appearance in social settings.

Adapt to the Occasion: Adjust your attire to match the specific occasion, reflecting your understanding of the event's nature and showing respect for fellow attendees. Being in sync with the occasion helps you feel more comfortable and confident in your interactions.

Comfort and Confidence: Choose outfits that adhere to the dress code while also making you feel comfortable and confident. Your self-assured appearance positively influences your social interactions, allowing you to engage more effectively with others.

Being Punctual and Considerate of Others' Time

Value Others' Time: Demonstrating respect for others' schedules by valuing their time is crucial in social interactions. Punctuality underscores your consideration for their commitments and contributes to a pleasant social experience.

Plan Ahead: Organize your schedule to ensure you can arrive on time for social events. Take into account factors like traffic, transportation options, and any necessary preparations to avoid unnecessary delays.

Communication in Case of Delay: If you anticipate a delay, communicate promptly with the host or other attendees. Transparency about delays not only shows respect for others' time but also helps manage expectations and minimize inconvenience.

Avoiding Overstaying: In casual get-togethers, it's essential to be mindful of the gathering's duration. Be considerate of others' time commitments, and if you notice that the event is winding down, gracefully make your exit to avoid overstaying your welcome.

Handling Seating Arrangements and Table Manners in Various Settings

Observing Social Cues: Pay close attention to social cues regarding seating arrangements. In more formal settings, wait for guidance on where to sit, whereas in casual settings, choose an appropriate seat. Respect for social cues ensures a smoother start to the event.

Table Manners and Digital Etiquette: Adhering to good table manners is essential. Use utensils correctly, engage in polite conversation, and be mindful of your surroundings. Remember that excusing yourself to take a phone call or staying off devices from messaging and scrolling through apps is considered best practice, ensuring that you maintain a respectful and pleasant dining experience for everyone. Good table manners and digital etiquette contribute to a positive dining experience for all those sharing the meal with you.

Adapting to Cultural Norms: In multicultural settings, it's considerate to acquaint yourself with basic cultural norms related to seating arrangements and table manners. This respect for diverse practices fosters a harmonious social environment and ensures that you're sensitive to the preferences of others.

Consideration for Dietary Preferences: When organizing events, take into account the dietary preferences and restrictions of your attendees. Choose venues that offer diverse menu options to accommodate varying tastes.

Managing Contributions in Potluck Events

Potluck events involve contributions from multiple participants, and coordinating these contributions requires thoughtful planning:

Coordinate Dishes: Organize a list of dishes to ensure various options. Communicate with participants to avoid duplicate dishes and create a balanced meal.

Consider Dietary Preferences: When signing up for potluck items, ask participants to indicate any dietary restrictions or preferences. This ensures that everyone can enjoy the dishes without concerns.

Provide Serving Utensils: Remind participants to bring serving utensils for their dishes. This ensures that everyone can easily access and enjoy the potluck offerings.

Create a Sign-Up Sheet: Use a sign-up sheet to track who's bringing what. This helps avoid last-minute surprises and allows for any necessary adjustments.

Communicate Clearly: Clearly communicate the potluck event's date, time, and location. Additionally, provide guidelines or themes to ensure a cohesive and enjoyable meal.

Plan for Allergies: Be mindful of allergies. Encourage participants to label their dishes with ingredients, especially if common allergens exist.

Express Appreciation: Finally, thank each participant for their contribution. Expressing appreciation creates a positive atmosphere and makes everyone feel valued.

Showing Appreciation to Event Hosts and Organizers

Hosting events and coordinating activities take effort, and showing appreciation to hosts and organizers is a thoughtful gesture:

Express Gratitude Verbally: A simple "thank you" goes a long way. To acknowledge the host's efforts, express your gratitude verbally during or after the event.

Send a Thank-You Note: Consider sending a handwritten or digital thank-you note highlighting what you enjoyed or found well-organized about the event.

Bring a Host Gift: If you're attending an event at someone's home, bringing a small gift, such as flowers, wine, or a thoughtful item, is a lovely gesture of appreciation.

Offer to Help: Offer assistance before, during, or after the event. Your willingness to contribute to setup, cleanup, or coordination is a valuable form of gratitude.

Share Positive Feedback: Share positive feedback with others who attended the event. Recognizing the host's efforts publicly reinforces the value of their work.

Donate to a Cause: If you know of a cause the host supports, consider donating as a meaningful way to show appreciation and contribute to something important to them.

Follow-up: Follow up with a message expressing gratitude once again after the event. This reinforces your appreciation and leaves a positive and lasting impression.

By following these guidelines, you can confidently navigate group social events, manage group dinners and potluck gatherings, and show appreciation to hosts and organizers with consideration and tact. These practices create a positive and harmonious social environment, making every social event a memorable and enjoyable experience."

Meeting Someone's Parents for the First Time

Prepare for the Occasion: Before meeting someone's parents, it's helpful to learn about their background and interests from your partner or friend. This can provide you with conversation topics and make a positive impression.

Dress Appropriately: Dressing well shows respect for the occasion and your hosts. It's usually a good idea to choose an outfit that's slightly more formal than what you'd wear in a casual setting.

Arrive on Time: Punctuality is crucial. Arriving on time demonstrates your reliability and respect for their schedule. If you anticipate being late, inform your partner or friend so they can relay the message.

Be Polite and Respectful: Always be polite and respectful to your host's parents. Address them by their titles (Mr. or Mrs.) unless they invite you to use their first names. Maintain good eye contact and offer a firm handshake when meeting them.

Engage in Conversation: Engage in friendly conversation to get to know them better. Ask about their interests, hobbies, and experiences. Be an active listener, showing genuine interest in what they say.

Avoid Controversial Topics: Steer clear of controversial or sensitive topics such as politics, religion, or personal matters. Keep the conversation light and positive.

Show Appreciation: Express gratitude for their hospitality and the opportunity to meet them. A simple "Thank you for having me" goes a long way in showing your appreciation.

Job Interviews

Research the Company: Before the interview, research the company thoroughly. Understand its mission, values, products, and services. This knowledge will help you tailor your responses during the interview.

Dress Professionally: Dress appropriately for the industry and company culture. When in doubt, it's better to be slightly overdressed than underdressed. A neat and professional appearance makes a strong first impression.

Arrive Early: Aim to arrive at the interview location about 10-15 minutes early. This demonstrates punctuality and gives you time to compose yourself before the interview.

Bring Necessary Documents: Carry multiple copies of your resume, a list of references, and any other relevant documents the employer may require. Having these readily available shows preparedness.

Practice Common Interview Questions: Prepare for common interview questions by practicing your responses. Focus on highlighting your skills, experiences, and how they align with the job requirements.

Ask Questions: Prepare thoughtful questions to ask the interviewer. This demonstrates your interest in the role and the company. Avoid asking questions about salary or benefits in the initial interview.

Body Language: Maintain positive body language throughout the interview. Offer a firm handshake, maintain eye contact, and sit up straight. Avoid fidgeting or appearing overly nervous.

Follow-Up: Send a thank-you email within 24 hours of the interview to express your appreciation for the opportunity and reiterate your interest in the position.

Sporting Events

Know the Rules and Teams: If you're attending a sporting event, familiarize yourself with the rules of the game and the teams that are playing. This will enhance your enjoyment and participation.

Respect Spectator Etiquette: Follow the spectator etiquette of the sport you're watching. This may include standing during certain moments, keeping noise levels appropriate, and refraining from disruptive behavior.

Cheer Responsibly: It's fine to cheer for your favorite team, but do so in a respectful manner. Avoid derogatory or offensive language directed at opposing teams or fans.

Respect Personal Space: Be mindful of personal space when seated in crowded areas. Avoid blocking others' views and allow them to enjoy the game.

Stay Safe: Follow safety guidelines provided by the venue. If attending with children, keep them under supervision and ensure their safety.

Clean Up After Yourself: Dispose of trash properly and keep the seating area clean. Leaving a mess is discourteous to others and the venue staff.

Engage in Friendly Banter: Good-natured banter with fans of the opposing team can be fun, but avoid confrontational or aggressive behavior. Remember, it's all in the spirit of the game.

Enjoy the Experience: Finally, remember that attending a sporting event is about having a good time. Enjoy the experience and savor the moments, win or lose.

Mastering Etiquette in Diverse Scenarios

In our social lives, we often find ourselves in unique and diverse etiquette scenarios, ranging from special occasions to unconventional situations. Navigating these scenarios gracefully requires thoughtfulness and understanding. Here's a comprehensive guide to etiquette in various scenarios, offering context and clarity to ensure your actions align with good manners.

Etiquette for Special Occasions

Weddings

- **RSVP Timely:** Respond to wedding invitations by the specified date.
- **Gifts**: If available, bring or send a gift even if you cannot attend, following the couple's registry.
- **Behavior:** During ceremonies and speeches, show respect and avoid excessive use of mobile devices.

Birthdays

- **Gifts:** Choose a thoughtful gift based on the recipient's preferences.
- **RSVP:** Promptly respond to birthday invitations.
- **Acknowledgment:** Express your gratitude for birthday gifts with a thank-you note or message.

Other Special Occasions

- **Anniversaries, Graduations, etc.:** Mark milestones with a thoughtful card or small gift as a sign of appreciation.

The Importance of Tipping in Service Industries

Understanding the ins and outs of tipping etiquette is a valuable skill as you navigate various service scenarios. Tipping is not just about courtesy; it's a way to express appreciation for the quality of service provided and ensure fair compensation in service industries. Whether you're dining out, using transportation services, enjoying spa treatments, or receiving services at home, knowing when and how to tip appropriately is essential. Let's explore why tipping matters and understand the specifics of tipping guidelines in different contexts.

Tipping Etiquette

Tipping serves several vital purposes:

Recognition of Service: Tipping serves as a tangible expression of gratitude and recognition for the dedication and quality of service provided by individuals in service industries. It's a way of saying "thank you" beyond just words.

Supplementing Income: In many professions within the service industry, like restaurants and salons, employees often rely on tips as a significant part of their income. Tipping ensures they receive fair compensation for their hard work.

Encouraging Excellence: Tipping is also a powerful motivator for service providers to excel in their roles. When they know their efforts are appreciated through tips, it encourages them to consistently deliver exceptional service and go the extra mile.

Cultural Norms: Tipping practices are deeply rooted in many cultures and are considered standard in various service sectors. Following local tipping customs not only shows respect for cultural traditions but also helps maintain social norms and expectations.

Tipping Guidelines for Various Services

Restaurants and Cafes: When dining in restaurants that offer table service, it's customary to tip between 15% and 20% of the total bill. Always check the bill for a service charge, as it might already be included.

Barbers and Salon Stylists: Tipping between 15% and 20% of the service cost is common practice in the beauty industry. Don't forget to tip shampoo assistants when appropriate.

Taxi Drivers: Tipping around 10% to 15% of the fare is the norm for taxi services. You might consider a higher tip for exceptional service or assistance with luggage.

Delivery Services: When receiving food or packages through delivery services, tipping between 10% and 20% of the total order is expected to appreciate the convenience and service provided.

Bartenders: It's common to tip bartenders $1 to $2 per drink or 15% to 20% of the total bill, especially in busy bars where bartenders work diligently to craft your beverages.

Valet Parking Attendants: Tipping $2 to $5 is generally suitable when using valet parking services, acknowledging their help in ensuring your vehicle's safe handling.

Masseuses and Spa Services: The standard guideline for tipping in spa settings is 15% to 20% of the service cost, though some establishments may include a service charge.

Wedding Services: Tipping is often expected for wedding services like photographers, musicians, and catering staff. Always refer to contracts and guidelines for each service provider to ensure you appreciate their hard work.

Delivery Services (Non-Food): When receiving non-food deliveries like furniture or appliances, tipping $5 to $10 per person is appreciated for the effort in safely transporting your items.

Handling Tipping When Receiving Home Services

Movers: Tipping each mover individually with a standard tip of $10 to $20 per mover for a service day is appropriate. For particularly challenging moves, consider a higher tip as a token of gratitude for their hard work.

Repair Services (Plumbers, Electricians): Tipping repair service providers $10 to $20 is thoughtful, especially for extensive work or exceptional effort in solving your household issues.

Landscapers and Gardeners: Tipping $20 to $50 per person at the end of the season or after a significant project is a common practice, recognizing the dedication they put into enhancing your outdoor space.

Cleaning Services: Tipping house cleaners 10% to 15% of the cleaning cost is appreciated, with adjustments based on the quality of service provided. It's a way to acknowledge their commitment to maintaining your living space.

Gratuities for Professional Services

Personal Trainers: While tipping personal trainers is optional, it can be a gesture of appreciation. Consider an amount often equivalent to one session's fee or a small gift to express your gratitude for their guidance and expertise.

Hair Stylists and Salon Services: When receiving additional services like washing hair or applying color, it's considerate to tip assistants $5 to $10 in addition to tipping for the salon services, recognizing their role in enhancing your salon experience.

Tutors and Coaches: Tipping for private tutors or coaches is optional but can be done as a token of appreciation, often equivalent to one session's fee, showing gratitude for their educational support and mentorship.

These are general tipping guidelines, and practices can vary depending on location, cultural norms, and personal preferences. Always take into account the quality of service when determining your tip amount. Tipping is a way to express gratitude, foster positive interactions, and acknowledge the hard work of those providing various services.

Gifting Etiquette for Holidays and Celebrations

Gift Exchanges: Clarify expectations for gift exchanges within social groups to ensure everyone is on the same page regarding gift-giving.

Hostess Gifts: Bring a small gift when attending holiday gatherings to express appreciation for the host's hospitality.

Holiday Cards: Use holiday cards to convey well wishes and sentiments to friends and loved ones during the holiday season.

App-Based Services

Ride-Sharing Services: Tip your driver through the app or with cash after a ride to appreciate their service and safe transportation.

Food Delivery: Consider tipping delivery drivers through the app or cash upon delivery as a token of gratitude for the convenience of having food delivered to your doorstep.

Service Ratings: Provide ratings and feedback to support service providers based on your experience, helping others make informed decisions.

Digital Transactions

E-Gifts: Show appreciation for online services with digital gift cards or e-gifts, making it easy to express gratitude for exceptional service.

Virtual Tips: Some platforms allow virtual tipping, a convenient way to express gratitude for exceptional service and support content creators or service providers.

Subscription Services

Cancellation Etiquette: Offer timely notice when canceling subscription services to help providers manage their business effectively and reduce any inconveniences.

Online Collaborations

Virtual Meetings: Practice good etiquette by muting your microphone when not speaking, dressing professionally, and minimizing background noise to ensure productive and respectful virtual interactions.

General Tips for Uncommon Situations

Research Local Customs: When in doubt about tipping or showing appreciation, research local customs to align with cultural norms and avoid unintentional misunderstandings.

Ask for Guidance: Don't hesitate to ask service providers or hosts about tipping practices or expectations if you are uncertain, ensuring your gestures are well-received and appropriate.

Consider Personal Relationships: Gauge the strength of your relationship with service providers when determining the appropriate level of tipping or showing appreciation to ensure your gestures are heartfelt and meaningful.

Express Gratitude: Regardless of the situation, expressing gratitude verbally or through a thank-you note amplifies the impact of your gesture and fosters goodwill in various social and service-related contexts.

Travel Etiquette: Navigating the Journey with Grace

Traveling is an adventure that takes us through various settings, from bustling airports to cozy hotels and unique vacation rentals. Ensuring a smooth and enjoyable experience for everyone involved requires understanding and practicing travel etiquette. This section will explore airport and travel etiquette, hotel and accommodation tipping, the art of tipping tour guides, and etiquette for staying in vacation rentals.

Airport and Travel Etiquette

Prepare for Security Checks:

- ▸ Remove items from your pockets and place them in the provided bins.

- Place liquids in a clear, quart-sized bag as per the regulations.
- Show respect for the space and privacy of fellow travelers while waiting in line and during security screening.

During Security Checks:

- Cooperate fully with security checks at airports.
- Be prepared to remove your shoes, belts, and items from your pockets.
- Follow instructions from security personnel diligently.
- Maintain a respectful demeanor throughout the security process.

Boarding Etiquette: Maintain order during boarding by adhering to designated boarding groups. Pay attention to the size of your carry-on and efficiently stow it in the overhead bin.

Seat Reclining: If your seat reclines, gradually consider the space behind you. Avoid reclining during meal service, and be attentive to the comfort of the person behind you.

In-Flight Courtesy:

- Mind noise levels, especially on nighttime flights.
- Use headphones when watching movies or listening to music.
- Refrain from using strong scents and be considerate of personal space.

Deplaning Etiquette: Wait your turn to deplane, following the row-by-row process. Exercise patience and allow those before you to exit the aircraft first.

Patience and Kindness: Recognize that travel can be stressful. Cultivate patience and extend kindness to fellow travelers, airport staff, and airline personnel. A positive attitude contributes to a more pleasant journey for everyone.

Tipping in Hotels and While Traveling

When it comes to tipping in hotels and during your travels, it's essential to understand the customs and practices to ensure a positive experience:

Housekeeping: Leaving a daily tip for housekeeping staff is a considerate gesture. You can choose to tip daily or at the end of your stay. Placing the tip in an envelope along with a note expressing your gratitude is a thoughtful touch.

Bellhops and Porters: When bellhops or porters assist with your luggage, it's customary to tip them between $2 to $5 per bag. The amount can vary based on the level of service they provide.

Concierge Services: Tipping for concierge services is discretionary but appreciated, especially if the concierge goes above and beyond to assist you. A tip ranging from $5 to $10 is appropriate for their efforts.

Room Service: When ordering room service, check your bill for any included service charges. If service charges are not included, consider leaving a 15% to 20% tip for the delivery.

Valet Parking Attendants: Tipping valet parking attendants is standard practice. When they return your car, it's customary to tip them between $2 to $5. Additional tips may be given for exceptional service.

Spa Services: Tipping for spa services can vary, so it's advisable to check if a service charge is already included. If not, a tip ranging from 15% to 20% of the service cost is customary.

Tipping Tour Guides and Local Services During Travel

Tour Guides: Show appreciation for tour guides by tipping them 10% to 15% of the tour cost. This amount can be adjusted based on the quality of the tour and the guide's expertise.

Local Transportation: When utilizing local drivers such as taxi drivers or rideshare services, tip according to local customs. Always check if a service charge is included in your fare.

Airport and Hotel Shuttle Drivers: When using shuttle services provided by hotels or airports, a tip of $2 to $5 per person is generally suitable.

Restaurant Service: Tipping in restaurants while traveling can vary widely by country. Before dining out, research the tipping norms at your travel destination to ensure that you tip appropriately.

These tipping practices can vary based on location, cultural norms, and personal preferences. Always consider the quality of service when determining your tip amount, and express your gratitude for the hard work of those providing various services during your travels.

Etiquette for Staying in Vacation Rentals

Communication with Hosts: Maintain clear and prompt communication with your hosts. Inform them of your arrival time and any special requests or requirements you may have.

Respect House Rules: Adhere to the house rules established by your host. These may include guidelines related to noise levels, smoking policies, and other considerations aimed at ensuring a harmonious stay.

Cleanliness:

1. Treat the vacation rental as you would your own space.
2. Leave it in the same or better condition than you found it.
3. Clean up after yourself and follow any specific instructions provided by the host.

Security and Privacy: Respect the security and privacy of the vacation rental. Always lock doors and windows when leaving, and avoid disturbing neighbors or fellow guests.

Check-Out Procedures: Follow the check-out procedures outlined by the host. This may include stripping beds, removing trash, or turning off appliances before departing.

Communication about Issues: If you encounter any issues during your stay, communicate with the host promptly and professionally. They can address concerns and ensure a more comfortable experience for you and future guests.

Review Thoughtfully: Leave a thoughtful and honest review for the vacation rental after your stay. Highlight positive aspects of your experience and provide constructive feedback, if necessary.

By adhering to these travel etiquette guidelines, you can navigate various travel settings with confidence and consideration for others. Practicing good travel etiquette enhances your journey, whether at the airport, staying in a hotel, exploring with a tour guide, or enjoying a vacation rental. It contributes to a positive travel experience for all.

Key Takeaways

Etiquette is About Respect and Consideration: Etiquette goes beyond rules; it's a way to show respect, consideration, and appreciation for others in various situations. Whether it's attending events, navigating unique scenarios, or engaging in the digital world, etiquette is your guide to positive interactions.

Effective Communication Strengthens Connections: Good etiquette includes responding to invitations and expressing gratitude, which helps strengthen connections with others. Be adaptable, as etiquette norms differ widely, and always be open to learning. Gratitude should be a constant companion, acknowledging acts of kindness and assistance.

Responsible and Thoughtful Actions Have Impact: Your responsible and thoughtful actions, like tipping service providers or respecting house rules, leave a lasting impact on those around you. Etiquette evolves with societal changes, so continue refining your skills as you grow. Embrace these principles to navigate life's intricate social tapestry with confidence and grace, making a positive impression on those you encounter.

Etiquette is a Lifelong Journey: Remember that etiquette is a lifelong journey. As society changes, so do etiquette norms. Stay open to evolving etiquette practices and adapt accordingly. Embracing these principles will empower you to navigate various social situations with poise and leave a positive mark on the people you meet.

Test Your Knowledge

1. What is one key purpose of etiquette in various scenarios?
   a. Following strict rules
   b. Demonstrating respect and consideration
   c. Showing off your knowledge
   d. Being the center of attention

2. When attending a wedding, what are the proper etiquette guidelines to follow?
   a. Ignore the invitation if you can't attend
   b. Bring a gift even if you can't attend
   c. Talk loudly during the ceremony
   d. Use your mobile phone to take pictures during speeches

3. Why is tipping for dining, deliveries, and personal care important in various cultures and industries?
   a. It helps service providers earn a fair income.
   b. It encourages exceptional service.
   c. It aligns with cultural norms.
   d. All of the above

4. What should you do when meeting someone's parents for the first time?
   a. Dress appropriately for the occasion.
   b. Be polite and use proper manners.
   c. Bring a small gift or token of appreciation.
   d. All of the above.

5. How can you express gratitude to service providers who offer exceptional service in the digital realm?
   a. Ignore their efforts
   b. Give them a low rating
   c. Provide virtual tips or positive feedback
   d. Complain about minor issues

CHAPTER 4

Financial Literacy

Financial literacy is a crucial skill, especially as you embark on a new chapter in your life. Take Brooklyn's story, for example. She had just moved out of her parents' house and was thrilled with her newfound independence. However, she was spending her money before taking care of her bills.

With her income stretched thin, Brooklyn found herself constantly behind on bills and struggling to make ends meet. Her plans to enjoy her newfound freedom turned into a constant battle with financial stress and constraints.

It was a wake-up call for Brooklyn. She realized the importance of financial literacy in managing her money effectively, saving for emergencies, and still having funds for fun. Determined to take control of her finances, she knew that financial literacy was her ticket to financial security, peace of mind, and the freedom to enjoy her independence without money worries.

Now that you've heard Brooklyn's financial journey, you might be wondering, "What exactly is financial literacy, and how can it help me avoid similar pitfalls?"

In this chapter, we'll delve deeper into the world of financial literacy. We'll explore what it means to be financially literate, why it's crucial for your future, and how it empowers you to make informed and responsible financial decisions. You'll discover practical aspects of managing your money, including budgeting, saving, and planning for a secure financial future.

Financial literacy isn't just about numbers and budgets; it's about gaining the knowledge and skills to navigate the complexities of personal finance successfully. So, if you want to avoid financial stress, achieve your goals, and relish the freedom that financial security brings, let's embark on this exciting journey of financial literacy. It's your key to unlocking a brighter and more secure future.

Budgeting and Money Management

Budgeting is a fundamental aspect of effective money management. It involves creating a plan for allocating your income to cover expenses, save, and achieve financial goals. Let's dive into personal finance, a topic of immense importance for young adults like you. Financial literacy is all about equipping yourself with the skills to make informed and responsible financial decisions, and it's never too early to start.

Creating a Personal Budget & Its Importance

A personal budget is like your financial GPS, mapping out your expected income and guiding you on allocating funds for various expenses, savings, and financial goals.

Here's how to get started:

Assess Your Income: Take a close look at all the money coming your way, whether it's your regular salary, income from a part-time job, or any other sources like freelancing or investments. Understanding your total income is the first step to managing your finances effectively. It allows you to see the full picture of what you have to work with each month.

List Your Expenses: Divide your expenses into two main categories: fixed and variable. Fixed expenses are the stable, recurring costs in your life, such as rent or mortgage payments, utility bills, and insurance premiums. On the other hand, variable expenses are the more flexible costs that can change from month to month, like dining out, entertainment, or shopping for clothes. This categorization helps you see where your money is consistently allocated and where it might fluctuate.

Identify Financial Goals: Take some time to think about your financial aspirations. What are your short-term goals, such as building an emergency fund or saving for a vacation? Equally important are your long-term goals, like planning for retirement or buying a home. Defining your goals gives you a clear direction and purpose for your financial decisions.

Allocate Funds: Once you've determined your income, listed your expenses, and identified your financial goals, it's time to create a plan. Allocate your income to different categories based on your priorities. This includes deciding how much you'll allocate for essentials like groceries, utilities, rent or mortgage, and transportation. Don't forget to allocate funds toward your savings goals as well. The key is to strike a balance between covering your needs and progressing toward your financial objectives without exceeding your income. This step ensures that you're actively working towards your goals and maintaining financial stability.

The importance of this budgeting exercise cannot be overstated:

Financial Awareness: Creating a budget shines a spotlight on where your money is going, providing you with a clear and honest view of your spending habits. This awareness is the first step in making informed financial decisions and identifying areas where you can cut back or make adjustments.

Goal Setting: Budgeting is a powerful tool for setting and achieving financial goals. Whether it's saving for a dream vacation, buying a new car, or building an emergency fund, a well-structured budget allows you to allocate resources strategically, making your financial aspirations more attainable.

Expense Control: One of the primary benefits of budgeting is that it puts you in the driver's seat when it comes to controlling your spending. With a budget in place, you can track your expenses and ensure that you're not overspending in any particular category. This control is essential for maintaining financial stability and avoiding unnecessary debt.

Emergency Preparedness: A comprehensive budget includes provisions for an emergency fund and a financial safety net. These funds are crucial for covering unexpected expenses, such as medical bills or car repairs, without derailing your overall financial plan. Budgeting ensures that you are prepared for life's uncertainties.

Debt Reduction: If you're dealing with debt, budgeting is an invaluable tool for developing a structured plan to pay it down. By allocating a portion of your income to debt repayment while still covering essential expenses, you can make steady progress towards becoming debt-free. Budgeting provides a roadmap for achieving financial freedom.

By following these steps and creating a personal budget, you'll be well on your way to mastering your finances, gaining control over your money, and achieving your financial goals. It's a practical and empowering skill that can lead to a more secure and prosperous future.

Fixed vs. Variable Expenses

Understanding the distinction between fixed and variable expenses is essential for effective budgeting and financial planning:

Fixed Expenses: Fixed expenses are the bedrock of your budget, representing consistent and predictable costs that remain relatively stable from month to month. These expenses are typically non-negotiable and include essential obligations such as:

- ▸ **Rent or Mortgage Payments:** Your monthly housing costs, whether you rent or own a home, are a prime example of a fixed expense. The amount you owe remains consistent unless you have a lease or mortgage rate adjustment.
- ▸ **Utilities:** Essential services like electricity, gas, water, and internet fall under fixed expenses. While the specific amounts might fluctuate slightly with usage, they are generally predictable.
- ▸ **Loan Payments:** If you have student loans, a car loan, or a mortgage, the monthly repayments constitute fixed expenses. These payments have predetermined amounts and due dates.
- ▸ **Insurance Premiums:** Monthly insurance premiums for health, auto, or renters' insurance are typically fixed. You'll know the exact amount you need to pay each month to maintain coverage.

Variable Expenses: Variable expenses, on the other hand, are more flexible and can vary significantly from one month to the next. These expenses encompass discretionary spending and lifestyle choices, including:

- **Groceries:** While groceries are a necessity, the amount you spend can fluctuate based on your meal planning, shopping habits, and dietary choices.
- **Dining Out:** Expenses related to dining at restaurants, cafes, or ordering takeout fall into the variable category. These costs can vary depending on your social activities and dining preferences.
- **Entertainment:** Variable expenses encompass entertainment activities such as going to the movies, attending concerts, or subscribing to streaming services beyond your fixed subscriptions.
- **Travel:** Any expenses related to travel, whether it's a weekend getaway or a vacation, are variable. Travel costs can vary widely based on the destination and the activities you choose.
- **Shopping and Personal Expenses:** Non-essential purchases, such as clothing, electronics, or personal grooming, are considered variable expenses. Your spending in this category depends on your wants and needs.

Understanding the difference between fixed and variable expenses is crucial for effective budgeting. Fixed expenses provide a stable foundation, while variable expenses offer flexibility. By categorizing your expenses in this way, you can prioritize essential financial obligations, allocate funds for savings and debt repayment, and make informed decisions about discretionary spending based on your financial goals and priorities.

Knowing how to manage both types is crucial for a balanced budget. Fixed expenses are non-negotiable, but with variable expenses, you have room for adjustments to align with your financial goals.

Mastering Your Spending Habits

Analyzing Expense Categories: To gain a comprehensive insight into your spending patterns, break down your expenses into distinct categories, such as groceries, dining out, entertainment, and utilities. This meticulous categorization provides a detailed understanding of precisely where your money is being allocated.

Setting Limits and Allocating Your Budget: Promote financial discipline by allocating specific amounts to different spending categories according to your financial goals and priorities. Setting spending limits not only fosters responsible budgeting but also assists in curbing unnecessary expenses that may hinder your financial progress.

Adjusting Spending Habits for Financial Alignment: Flexibility is key to financial success. Identify areas where your spending habits can be adjusted to better align with your financial goals. This could involve making conscious efforts to reduce discretionary spending or seeking more cost-effective alternatives for certain expenditures.

Prioritizing Essential Needs Over Non-Essential Wants: Conduct a critical assessment of your expenses by distinguishing between needs and wants. Prioritize fulfilling essential needs while maintaining mindfulness regarding discretionary spending on non-essential wants. This practice ensures that you allocate your resources thoughtfully and in alignment with your financial objectives.

Integrating Financial Goals with Budgeting

Let's put your financial goals on the map of your budget.

Spread the Wealth: Allocate specific portions of your budget to different financial goals, ensuring that your hard-earned money goes where it matters most.

Regular Review: Life isn't static, and neither are your goals. Review and adjust your budget allocations periodically based on evolving circumstances, income fluctuations, and changing financial objectives.

Priority Alert: Don't forget the golden rule of budgeting - your emergency fund is your safety net, so make it a priority.

The Necessity of an Emergency Fund

An emergency fund is like a financial safety net, providing you with a buffer against unexpected expenses or financial setbacks. Here's why it's crucial:

Financial Security: An emergency fund offers financial security, reducing stress and anxiety during challenging times. It prevents you from relying on credit cards or loans to cover unforeseen costs.

Unpredictable Emergencies: Life is full of surprises, and many situations can't be foreseen. Emergencies could include medical expenses, car repairs, home repairs, or sudden job loss. Having an emergency fund means you're prepared for these unexpected events.

Defining a Genuine Financial Emergency

Not all unexpected expenses qualify as genuine financial emergencies. It's essential to differentiate between true emergencies and regular, albeit unexpected, costs:

Genuine Emergencies: These are unforeseen and necessary expenses that, if left unaddressed, could have severe consequences. Examples include medical emergencies, urgent home repairs (e.g., a leaking roof), or unexpected job loss.

Non-Emergencies: Regular, irregular, or optional expenses, like car maintenance, vacations, or holiday shopping, are not genuine emergencies. While they may be unexpected, they can be budgeted for separately.

Determining the Right Amount for Your Emergency Fund

The size of your emergency fund depends on your individual circumstances, but there are some general guidelines to consider. To get you started, aim to save at least $1000 to always have available at your disposal.

Basic Starter Emergency Fund: Financial experts often recommend starting with a basic emergency fund that covers essential living expenses for three to six months. This includes rent or mortgage, utilities, groceries, transportation, and insurance premiums. Having this fund in place provides a good foundation for financial stability.

Building a Solid Emergency Fund: Over time, aim to build your emergency fund to cover living expenses for six to nine months or even up to one year.

This extended cushion offers added peace of mind and protection against more prolonged financial challenges, such as extended unemployment.

Consider Personal Factors: Adjust the size of your emergency fund based on your specific situation. Factors like job stability, health, and family circumstances may influence the amount you need. For example, those with irregular income or dependents may want a larger fund.

Savings Milestones: You don't need to save the full amount all at once. Set milestones and gradually work towards your goal. Even having a small emergency fund initially is better than none at all.

In summary, an emergency fund is a financial lifeline that provides stability and peace of mind during unexpected situations. It's crucial to distinguish between real emergencies and regular expenses and save an amount that aligns with your unique financial situation and goals. Building a solid emergency fund is a fundamental step toward financial security and resilience.

Side Hustles and Additional Income

In today's dynamic world, many individuals are turning to side hustles to boost their income and pursue their passions. Whether you're looking to pay off debt, save for a dream vacation, or simply increase your financial flexibility, side hustles offer a valuable opportunity to amplify your earnings. In this chapter, we'll explore the ins and outs of side hustles, from identifying your skills and interests to effectively managing your time and resources, helping you embark on a successful journey toward financial growth and fulfillment.

Recognizing Your Income Potential

If you're eager to boost your income, you can tap into your unique skills, hobbies, and passions. Here's how to get started:

Identifying Your Strengths and Interests

What Are You Good At?: Begin by assessing your strengths and skills. Identify areas where you excel, whether it's teaching, writing, crafting, or a particular hobby. Your innate talents can be the foundation for a successful side hustle.

Passion Projects: Beyond your skills, consider what you're passionate about. Pursuing a side hustle related to your interests can be fulfilling and motivating. It can also help you stay committed and enjoy the journey.

Market Research and Positioning

Market Savvy: Before diving in, research the demand for your chosen side hustle in your local area or online marketplaces. Understanding market needs and competition will help you position your services effectively. Look for gaps in the market or ways to differentiate yourself.

Time Management and Flexibility

Time Check: Assess how much time you can realistically dedicate to your side hustle. It's crucial to strike a balance between your primary job, personal life, and your new income-generating endeavor. Flexibility is essential, as it allows you to adapt to changing circumstances.

Exploring Side Hustle Ideas

Inspiration Station: The world of side hustles is vast and diverse. Explore a range of ideas, from dog walking to tutoring, freelancing in various fields, or selling handmade crafts. The key is to find an option that resonates with you and aligns with your skills and interests.

Evaluate Viability: While brainstorming ideas, evaluate their viability and income potential. Consider factors like startup costs, required equipment or resources, and the potential return on investment. Some side hustles may require minimal upfront expenses, making them more accessible.

Starting Small and Scaling

Begin Small: It's okay to start small with your side hustle. Begin by offering your services to friends and family or on a small scale. This allows you to refine your offerings, gain experience, and build a client base gradually.

Scaling Up: As your side hustle gains traction and you become more comfortable, explore opportunities to scale up your business. This might involve increasing your client base, expanding your services, or investing in marketing to reach a broader audience.

Financial Planning and Goals

Set Financial Goals: Clearly define your financial goals for your side hustle. Whether it's paying off debt, building an emergency fund, or saving for a specific purpose, having clear objectives will keep you motivated.

Budget and Taxes: Keep track of your side hustle income and expenses to ensure you're financially responsible. Understand the tax implications of your side hustle and plan accordingly.

Remember that starting a side hustle requires dedication, effort, and a willingness to learn. It's an opportunity to not only increase your income but also explore your passions and interests while enhancing your financial well-being.

Balancing Your Checkbook and Avoiding Overdrafts

Balancing your checkbook is a fundamental practice in personal finance that forms the bedrock of financial accuracy and stability. This section explores why balancing your checkbook matters, walks you through a step-by-step guide, introduces useful tools and apps, and delves into critical aspects of responsible checking account management.

Why Balance Your Checkbook?

Balancing your checkbook is a crucial financial practice for several reasons:

Accuracy and Awareness: Balancing your checkbook ensures that your recorded transactions align precisely with your bank's records, accurately representing your available funds. It's akin to a financial reality check.

Detecting Errors: Beyond mere accuracy, regular reconciliation of your checkbook helps you become your financial detective. It's your means of identifying any discrepancies or errors in your financial transactions, enabling you to address and correct them promptly.

Preventing Overdrafts: Overdrafts are like financial potholes—they can cause a bumpy ride. You can avoid overdrawing your account by keeping an accurate account of your transactions. Overdrafts can result in fees and other unpleasant financial consequences, so avoiding them at all costs is wise.

Step-by-Step Guide to Balancing Your Checkbook

Record Transactions Promptly: A timely recording of all transactions is the foundation of a balanced checkbook. Whether it's checks, deposits, or debit card transactions, be diligent in entering them into your checkbook register as soon as they occur. This ensures accuracy and helps you stay aware of your spending in real-time.

Compare with Bank Statements: Regularly compare your checkbook register with your monthly bank statements. It's the financial equivalent of double-checking your homework. Verify that the transactions in both records match and are accurately reflected. If you spot discrepancies, don't fret; we'll address them shortly.

Reconcile Monthly: At the close of each month, it's time to reconcile your checkbook with your bank statement. This involves ensuring that your register's ending balance perfectly matches the statement's ending balance. The goal? A harmonious financial symphony.

Address Discrepancies: While rare, discrepancies can occasionally sneak in. If you discover differences between your records and the bank statement, don't ignore them. Investigate and resolve these issues promptly. It may involve reaching out to the bank or reviewing your receipts to pinpoint the source of the discrepancy.

Balancing Tools and Apps

Checkbook Register Apps: In our digital age, we have tools at our fingertips to make this process more convenient. Consider using digital checkbook register apps like Goodbudget, PocketGuard, or even dedicated banking apps offered by your financial institution. These apps simplify the input and tracking of transactions, allowing you to maintain financial accuracy.

Budgeting Software: Broaden your financial horizons by exploring budgeting software such as YNAB (You Need A Budget) or Mint. These versatile tools help track expenses and facilitate overall financial management, keeping your financial house in order.

Avoiding Overdrafts and Managing Your Checking Account

Overdraft fees are the stealthy financial predators that pounce when you spend more money than is available in your checking account. These fees can vary by bank but typically range from $30 to $40 or even more for each overdraft occurrence. When multiple transactions occur without sufficient funds, these fees can add up quickly, leading to significant unexpected expenses.

Tips for Avoiding Overdrafts:

- ▸ **Regularly Check Your Balance:** Staying informed about your account balance is your financial compass, guiding you away from rocky financial waters. Make it a habit to check your balance regularly, whether through your bank's website, mobile app, or ATMs.
- ▸ **Set Up Alerts:** Take advantage of modern banking features that allow you to stay vigilant effortlessly. Enable account alerts that notify you when your balance drops below a specified threshold. These alerts act like a financial guardian angel on your shoulder, giving you timely warnings to avoid overdrafts.
- ▸ **Opt-Out of Overdraft Protection:** While it may sound counterintuitive, consider opting out of overdraft protection. This option prevents transactions that exceed your balance from going through, acting as a safety net to prevent costly missteps. Without overdraft protection, if you attempt a transaction with insufficient funds, it will be declined rather than processed with an overdraft fee.

Managing Overdraft Protection: It's important to note that if you have overdraft protection, it's not a free pass. Overdraft protection typically means that your bank covers the transaction temporarily, allowing it to go through even if you don't have enough funds. However, you'll need to pay back the overdraft amount promptly. This means that you'll need to bring your account balance back to a positive level, often within a short time frame, to avoid additional fees and potential account closure.

By being aware of the costs associated with overdrafts, monitoring your account balance, setting up alerts, and making informed decisions about overdraft protection, you can effectively manage your checking account and avoid unnecessary expenses.

Managing Your Checking Account Responsibly

Managing Your Checking Account Responsibly

Managing your checking account effectively involves not only balancing your checkbook but also understanding the various ways to pay your bills. Let's explore different payment methods and their pros and cons:

Automatic Payments (Auto Withdrawals):

- Pros:
  - Convenience: Set it and forget it. Automatic payments save time and ensure bills are paid on time.
  - Timely Payments: Eliminates the risk of late payments and associated fees.
  - Consistency: Payments are made regularly, helping you maintain a positive payment history.
- Cons:
  - Lack of Control: Auto withdrawals can become a blind spot if not monitored. You may overlook changes in billing amounts or unauthorized charges.
  - Overdraft Risk: Until you're financially literate, auto withdrawals can be risky, potentially leading to overdrafts if you forget to account for them.

Manual Payments (Writing Checks or Online Payments):

- Pros:
    - Control: You have complete control over when and how much you pay.
    - Awareness: Manual payments require you to actively engage with your finances, promoting financial awareness.
    - Flexibility: You can adjust payment amounts based on your financial situation.
- **Cons:**
    - Time-Consuming: Manual payments can be more time-consuming than automatic ones.
    - Potential for Late Payments: If not managed well, manual payments may lead to late fees.

Paying by Phone:

- **Pros:**
    - Convenience: Paying by phone offers flexibility and convenience.
    - Immediate Confirmation: You receive immediate confirmation of your payment.
- **Cons:**
    - Security Risks: Phone payments can pose security risks if not done through secure channels.
    - May Incur Service Fees: Some service providers may charge convenience fees for phone payments.

Additional Tips for Managing Your Checking Account Responsibly:

Monitor Automatic Payments: While automatic payments are convenient, keep a watchful eye on these transactions to avoid unexpected deductions.

Review Statements: Regularly reviewing your bank statements is a prudent practice. It helps you promptly catch any unauthorized transactions or errors, giving you the power to rectify them.

Secure Personal Information: In this age of digital transactions, safeguarding your checkbook, debit card, and personal information is vital. These safeguards prevent fraud and ensure your financial security.

By understanding the pros and cons of different payment methods and adopting responsible practices, you'll not only balance your checkbook but also balance your financial life, taking steps toward stability, accuracy, and peace of mind.

The Importance of an Emergency Credit Card

In life's unpredictable journey, unexpected expenses like medical emergencies, car repairs, or urgent home fixes can catch us off guard. An emergency credit card serves as your reliable financial safety net, offering unparalleled convenience when immediate cash is unavailable. Beyond convenience, responsible use of such a card also helps build a strong credit history, a vital foundation for future financial endeavors.

Obtaining and Managing an Emergency Credit Card

Choosing the Right Card: When navigating the world of credit cards, remember that one size doesn't fit all. It's crucial to select a credit card that suits your specific financial needs and creditworthiness. Hunt for a card that offers favorable terms, low interest rates, and minimal fees. Much like choosing the perfect tool for a job, this decision can significantly impact your financial stability.

Credit Limit Considerations: Your credit limit plays a pivotal role in your financial safety net. Ensure it's set at a level that can adequately cover potential emergency expenses, but exercise caution not to overextend yourself. Finding that sweet spot where your credit limit aligns with your repayment capacity is essential for responsible credit card use.

Read the Terms and Conditions: The fine print holds the key to understanding your credit card agreement. Dive into the terms and conditions, scrutinizing interest rates, fees, and any rewards or benefits tied to the card. Knowledge is your financial armor, empowering you to make informed decisions and avoid potential pitfalls.

Using Sparingly: While your emergency credit card can be a lifeline during unexpected financial crises, it's important to adhere to the golden rule: reserve it for genuine emergencies, not everyday expenses or discretionary spending. Remember, it's not an extra wallet but your financial safety rope, ready to support you when you need it most.

Making On-Time Payments and Responsible Usage

Responsible Credit Card Usage and Avoiding Debt: A credit card is a powerful financial tool, offering convenience, safety in emergencies, and potential rewards like cashback or travel points. However, it also carries the risk of debt if not used responsibly. The cardinal rule of credit card usage is to charge only what you can pay off in full each month, preventing the cycle of debt.

Importance of Full Payments: To avoid the debt trap, always aim to pay off your credit card balance entirely each month. This practice keeps you within your means and prevents interest charges from accumulating. Essentially, you're using your credit card as a financial tool rather than a source of long-term debt.

Avoiding Cash Advances and Monitoring Statements: Cash advances from your credit card can be like quicksand, easy to sink into and challenging to escape due to higher interest rates and additional fees. Reserve this option strictly for genuine emergencies. Regularly monitoring your credit card statements is essential; they serve as your financial mirror, reflecting your spending habits and account activity. This practice helps you stay informed about your spending and promptly identify any unauthorized transactions, acting as your financial GPS toward security and peace of mind.

Building and Maintaining Good Credit

Maintaining a consistent and responsible approach to credit card usage is essential for building a positive credit history, which acts as your financial passport. Strive for balance by keeping credit card balances low in relation to your credit limit, with a target credit utilization ratio below 30%. This demonstrates responsible credit use and strengthens your credit score. Furthermore, avoid closing old credit card accounts, as the length of your credit history significantly impacts your credit score. Think of these older accounts as financial elders, offering wisdom and stability to your credit profile.

Understanding Credit Scores, Debt, and Building Good Credit

Understanding Credit Scores: Credit scores are like your financial report card, influencing various aspects of your financial life. They are calculated using factors such as payment history, credit utilization, length of credit history, types of credit in use, and new credit applications. Taking the time to comprehend these factors can empower you to make informed decisions about your credit.

Managing Debt Responsibly: Responsible credit management is crucial for avoiding the pitfalls of excessive debt. Accumulating high levels of debt relative to your credit limit can negatively impact your credit score. Finding the right balance between credit utilization and debt management is key to maintaining a healthy financial profile.

Building Good Credit Habits: Cultivating good credit habits is akin to tending to a growing plant. It involves consistently paying bills on time, avoiding maxing out credit cards, and regularly reviewing your credit report for errors or discrepancies. These daily financial practices contribute to a positive credit history and a strong credit score, opening doors to various financial opportunities.

What is a Credit Score?

A credit score is your financial fingerprint—a numerical representation of your creditworthiness. It condenses your credit history and financial behavior into a three-digit number. Consider it a quick assessment for lenders, gauging your loan repayment likelihood.

Building and Maintaining Your Credit Score

Establishing Credit: If you're new to credit, it's essential to take deliberate steps to establish your credit history. This can be achieved by obtaining a credit card, securing a small loan, or becoming an authorized user on someone else's credit account. Think of it as laying the first brick in building your financial castle. These initial credit endeavors provide you with the opportunity to demonstrate your creditworthiness and begin constructing a robust financial profile that will serve you well in the future.

Timely Payments: The heartbeat of your credit score is punctual payments. To maintain a healthy credit history and boost your credit score, it's crucial to consistently pay all your bills, loans, and credit card payments on time. Timely payments not only establish a rhythm of financial responsibility but also reflect positively on your creditworthiness.

Credit Mix: Maintaining a diverse mix of credit types can have a positive impact on your credit score. This mix typically includes credit cards, installment loans (like auto loans or personal loans), and retail accounts (store credit cards). Demonstrating your ability to manage various types of credit responsibly showcases your financial versatility and can enhance your creditworthiness in the eyes of lenders.

Credit Utilization: Your credit utilization ratio plays a significant role in your credit score. To maintain a favorable credit utilization ratio, it's advisable to keep your credit card balances low relative to your credit limits. A low credit utilization ratio demonstrates your judicious use of available credit, indicating to creditors that you're not relying heavily on borrowed funds and are capable of managing your credit responsibly.

Key Takeaways

- **Budgeting is Key:** Establishing and sticking to a budget is the foundation of financial literacy. It provides the roadmap for managing your income, expenses, and savings.
- **Emergency Preparedness:** Building an emergency fund and having an emergency credit card are vital aspects of financial security. They offer protection and peace of mind during unforeseen circumstances.
- **Credit and Debt Management:** Responsible use of credit cards, understanding credit scores, and managing debt are essential for a healthy financial future. These practices pave the way for better financial opportunities.

▸ **Financial Goals Matter:** Setting clear financial goals and following the SMART criteria helps you prioritize and achieve your objectives. It ensures your resources are directed toward what matters most to you.

▸ **Protecting Your Financial Identity:** Safeguarding your personal and financial information, monitoring your credit, and being cautious online are crucial steps to avoid identity theft and maintain financial stability.

By mastering these key principles of financial literacy, you'll be better equipped to make informed financial decisions, achieve your goals, and build a secure and prosperous future.

Test Your Knowledge

1. What is the primary purpose of creating a personal budget?
    a. To track your favorite TV shows
    b. To plan your vacation
    c. To manage your income and expenses
    d. To learn a new language
2. Why is it important to make on-time payments for your credit card bills?
    a. Because it's fun
    b. Because it impresses your friends
    c. Because it helps build and maintain a positive credit history
    d. Because it's required by law
3. What is the significance of an emergency fund?
    a. It acts as a vacation fund
    b. It provides a financial safety net for unexpected expenses
    c. It's a fund for luxury shopping
    d. It helps you invest in the stock market
4. Which of the following is NOT a factor that affects your credit score?
    a. Payment history
    b. Credit utilization

   c. Length of credit history

   d. Your favorite color

5. What is the recommended credit utilization ratio for maintaining a positive credit score?

   a. Over 50%

   b. Exactly 30%

   c. Below 30%

   d. It doesn't matter

6. Which of the following is NOT a step in balancing your checkbook?

   a. Recording all transactions promptly

   b. Avoiding checking your bank statements

   c. Comparing your checkbook register with your bank statements

   d. Reconciling your checkbook with your bank statement monthly

7. Which of the following is NOT a strategy for managing debt?

   a. Creating a structured repayment plan

   b. Prioritizing high-interest debts

   c. Negotiating with creditors

   d. Accumulating new debt regularly

CHAPTER 5

Independent Living

Imagine this: you're in control, making your own choices, and embracing the exciting challenges of life on your terms. Independent living is your chance to break free, but it comes with responsibilities, from managing your own space to handling your finances. This guide is your ticket to mastering the art of independent living and enjoying the freedom you've been waiting for.

Allow me to introduce you to Sarah, a young adult who recently embarked on her journey into independent living. Sarah was thrilled to move into her very own apartment, a place she had fallen in love with at first sight. It was spacious, in a great location, and had all the features she ever dreamed of. However, there was one tiny detail she hadn't fully considered: the cost.

Sarah soon realized that the apartment of her dreams came with a price tag that stretched her budget to its limits. Between rent, utilities, and other expenses, she found herself struggling to make ends meet. To make matters more challenging, her daily commute to work was about an hour each way, putting additional wear and tear on her car and increasing her fuel costs.

In the beginning, Sarah relied heavily on fast food for her meals due to her busy schedule and lack of cooking skills. But as the bills started piling up, she knew she needed to find a more cost-effective way to take care of herself.

With determination and a desire to master the art of independent living, Sarah decided to tackle her financial challenges head-on. She began by creating a budget to track her expenses and started learning how to cook simple, budget-friendly meals at home.

Sarah didn't stop there. She got clever with her commute and discovered that she had a coworker who lived not too far away. They decided to take turns commuting together, which not only saved Sarah money but also made her daily journey much more enjoyable.

By making these changes, Sarah was not only able to save money but also improve her overall well-being. She discovered that cooking her meals was not only cost-effective but also healthier and more satisfying.

When her lease finally came to an end, Sarah had learned valuable lessons about budgeting, the importance of making informed decisions when it came to housing, and the benefits of finding creative solutions to everyday challenges. She embarked on a new apartment hunt, this time with a more realistic budget in mind. She found a place that was the right size, at the right price, and still conveniently located.

Sarah's journey into independent living had its share of challenges, but it also taught her the importance of financial literacy, budgeting, and making choices that align with her goals and resources. As you read on, you'll gain insights into these essential life skills, helping you navigate your own path to independence with confidence and success.

Choosing the Right Place for You

Evaluate Your Finances: Take a thorough look at your financial situation, including income, savings, and monthly expenses. Determine the amount you can comfortably allocate to rent without compromising other essential needs.

Consider Additional Costs: Beyond rent, account for expenses like utilities, internet, groceries, and transportation. This comprehensive budgeting approach ensures you have a realistic understanding of your financial commitments.

The 30% Rule: A common guideline is to spend no more than 30% of your monthly income on rent. This helps maintain a healthy balance between housing costs and overall financial well-being.

Location

Proximity to Work or School: Choose a convenient location for commuting to work or school. Consider the time and cost associated with transportation.

Neighborhood Safety: Research the safety of potential neighborhoods. Online resources, local crime statistics, and talking to current residents can provide valuable insights.

Amenities and Services: Assess the proximity of essential services and amenities, such as grocery stores, medical facilities, public transportation, and recreational areas.

Community Vibes: Spend time in the neighborhood to feel its atmosphere. Consider your preferences regarding urban or suburban living, noise levels, and community activities.

Apartment Hunting Tips

Start your apartment search well in advance to have ample time for research and visits.

Use Online Platforms: Explore online rental platforms, real estate websites, and apps to browse available listings. These platforms often provide filters to refine your search based on preferences.

Attend Open Houses: Physically inspect potential apartments by attending open houses. This allows you to assess the condition of the property and its surroundings.

Bring a Checklist: Create a checklist of essential features and requirements. Use it during apartment visits to ensure that the property meets your criteria.

Ask Questions: Don't hesitate to ask the landlord or property manager questions about the lease, maintenance, and any specific concerns you may have.

Understanding Lease Agreements

Read Thoroughly: Carefully read the entire lease agreement before signing. Pay attention to clauses regarding rent, lease duration, maintenance responsibilities, and any penalties for breaking the lease.

Clarify Ambiguities: Seek clarification on any ambiguous or confusing terms within the lease. It's crucial to clearly understand your rights and obligations as a tenant.

Security Deposit Details: Understand the terms related to the security deposit, including the amount, conditions for its return, and any deductions that may be made.

Lease Duration: Confirm the duration of the lease and any provisions related to renewals or termination. Understand the penalties for breaking the lease early.

Document Property Condition: Document the property's current condition before moving in. Take photos or videos and make notes. This can be valuable when discussing security deposit refunds at the end of the lease.

Organizing and Maintaining Your Space

Declutter Regularly: Keeping your living space clutter-free isn't just about aesthetics; it also contributes to a more organized and peaceful environment. Regularly go through your belongings, and if you come across items you no longer need or use, consider donating or selling them. By doing this, you'll not only maintain a tidy living space but also free up valuable room for activities and storage.

Storage Solutions: Efficient storage is a game-changer in independent living. Invest in shelves, bins, and organizers to maximize your living space and keep your belongings neatly arranged. By having a designated place for everything, you'll reduce clutter and make it easier to find what you need when you need it.

Create a Cleaning Schedule: Establishing a cleaning schedule is a key part of adulting. It ensures that no corner of your home gets neglected. Create a routine that includes daily tasks like doing the dishes and tidying up, as well as weekly chores like vacuuming and dusting. Having a schedule helps you stay on top of housekeeping and maintain a clean and inviting living space.

Personalization: Your living space should reflect your personality and make you feel comfortable. Add personal touches through decor, artwork, or furnishings that resonate with you. Personalization not only enhances the aesthetics of your home but also contributes to your overall well-being by creating a space that feels uniquely yours.

Cleaning and Housekeeping Tips

Daily Maintenance: Incorporate daily cleaning habits into your routine. Simple tasks like washing dishes immediately after meals, wiping down surfaces, and making your bed each morning can go a long way in keeping your living space clean and organized. Consistency with these small tasks makes daily maintenance easier.

Weekly Cleaning: Designate specific days for deeper cleaning. On these days, focus on tasks like vacuuming, mopping, dusting, and cleaning the bathroom. Regular weekly cleaning prevents dirt and grime from building up and ensures a more hygienic environment.

Cleaning Supplies: Keep essential cleaning supplies readily available. Stock up on items like all-purpose cleaners, sponges, microfiber cloths, and trash bags. Having these supplies on hand ensures that you can quickly tackle cleaning tasks as they arise, making the process more efficient.

Home Repairs and Maintenance

Learn Basic Repairs: Basic home repair skills can save you time and money. Familiarize yourself with tasks like fixing a leaky faucet, changing light bulbs, and unclogging drains. Having these skills allows you to address common issues independently and avoid calling in professionals for minor repairs.

Create a Maintenance Calendar: Develop a maintenance calendar to keep track of important tasks. This includes changing air filters, testing smoke detectors, and servicing appliances. Regular maintenance not only extends the lifespan of your home systems but also helps prevent major issues that can be costly to fix.

Emergency Preparedness: Being prepared for emergencies is a crucial aspect of independent living. Know how to shut off utilities like water and gas in case of emergencies. Keep a basic toolkit with essential tools for quick fixes. Additionally, have a list of emergency contacts readily available. Quick action during emergencies can minimize damage and ensure your safety.

Landlord Communication: Maintain open and prompt communication with your landlord regarding any necessary repairs or maintenance issues. Report problems as soon as they arise to ensure a safe and functional living environment. Timely reporting can also help you build a positive relationship with your landlord.

Sharing Responsibilities with Roommates

Establish Clear Expectations: Effective communication is key when sharing living spaces with roommates. Have open discussions about expectations regarding cleanliness, shared expenses, and how responsibilities will be divided. Clarity from the beginning helps prevent misunderstandings and conflicts down the road.

Create a Chore Chart: To ensure fairness and transparency in household chores, consider developing a chore chart that clearly outlines each person's responsibilities. Rotate tasks regularly so that no one feels burdened, and everyone contributes equally to maintaining a clean and organized living space.

Hold Regular Meetings: Maintaining a harmonious living environment with roommates requires ongoing communication. Schedule periodic roommate meetings to discuss any concerns, adjustments to responsibilities, or changes in the living situation. These meetings provide a platform for addressing issues promptly and collaboratively.

Respect Each Other's Space: While shared living spaces come with their benefits, it's important to respect each other's privacy and personal space. Establish guidelines for shared spaces and set boundaries as needed. Mutual respect for one another's space is fundamental to peaceful cohabitation and positive relationships with roommates.

By following these guidelines and fostering open communication, you can effectively manage your household, maintain a clean and organized living space, and cultivate positive relationships with your roommates. This approach ensures a comfortable and enjoyable experience in independent living.

Cooking and Meal Planning

Cooking and meal planning are essential skills for independent living, contributing to a healthier lifestyle and better financial management. This comprehensive guide will help you develop these vital skills, allowing you to create nutritious and diverse meals while staying within your budget. Let's dive deeper into each topic:

Basic Cooking Skills and Techniques

Knife Skills: Mastering fundamental knife skills, such as chopping, dicing, and mincing, not only improves your efficiency in the kitchen but also ensures your safety as you handle sharp utensils.

Cooking Methods: Familiarize yourself with various cooking methods like sautéing, roasting, boiling, steaming, and baking. Each method offers unique flavors and textures to your dishes, adding variety to your meals.

Temperature Control: Understand the significance of temperature control, especially when cooking proteins. Using a food thermometer to ensure meats reach the recommended internal temperature for safe consumption is crucial for your well-being.

Seasoning and Flavoring: Experiment with herbs, spices, and flavorings to elevate the taste of your dishes. Learning how to balance flavors and use seasonings effectively will allow you to create delicious meals with your unique touch.

Grocery Shopping on a Budget

Create a Shopping List: Plan your weekly meals and create a shopping list based on the necessary ingredients. Sticking to your list will help you avoid impulsive and unplanned purchases, saving you money in the long run.

Buy in Bulk: Consider buying non-perishable items like rice, pasta, and canned goods in bulk. This cost-effective approach can significantly reduce your grocery expenses over time.

Explore Generic Brands: Don't hesitate to try generic or store-brand products. They are often more budget-friendly than name brands while maintaining good quality.

Shop Seasonally: Opt for seasonal fruits and vegetables, as they are usually more abundant and affordable. Embracing seasonal produce not only helps you save money but also adds variety to your diet.

Meal Planning for a Healthy Diet

Balanced Meals: Aim for balanced meals that incorporate proteins, carbohydrates, healthy fats, and a generous portion of fruits and vegetables. A well-rounded diet promotes overall health and well-being.

Portion Control: Practice portion control to prevent overeating. Using smaller plates and bowls can naturally regulate your portion sizes and assist in maintaining a healthy weight.

Meal Prepping: Embrace meal prepping by preparing ingredients in advance or cooking meals for the week. This time-saving technique ensures you have healthy options readily available and reduces the temptation to order takeout on busy days.

Diverse Protein Sources: Incorporate a variety of protein sources into your diet, such as lean meats, poultry, fish, beans, legumes, and plant-based alternatives. Diverse protein choices provide essential nutrients and keep your meals interesting.

Preparing Meals at Home

Plan Weekly Menus: Organize your weekly menus while considering your schedule and available cooking time. This approach streamlines your grocery shopping and meal preparation processes, making your life easier.

Batch Cooking: Consider batch cooking and storing leftovers for future meals. This efficient method saves you time and reduces the need for daily cooking, allowing you to enjoy a home-cooked meal even on busy days.

Explore New Recipes: Keep your meals exciting and diverse by experimenting with new recipes. Explore the vast array of options available online and in cookbooks to discover new flavors and cooking techniques.

Mindful Eating: Cultivate mindful eating habits by savoring your meals without distractions. This practice promotes a healthier relationship with food, enhances your appreciation for flavors, and can aid in weight management.

With these insights and practical tips, you'll be well-equipped to develop your cooking skills, shop smartly on a budget, and maintain a nutritious and satisfying diet at home, all while expanding your culinary horizons. Happy cooking!

Car Insurance

Car insurance is an indispensable component of responsible car ownership that offers vital financial protection in case of accidents or damage to your vehicle. Understanding car insurance is essential for young adults, as it provides security and is mandated by law in many states. In this guide, we'll delve deeper into the importance of car insurance, its various types, and how to select coverage that suits your needs and budget.

Why Car Insurance Matters

Car insurance is much more than a legal requirement; it's a financial safeguard and a source of peace of mind.

Financial Safeguard: Car insurance acts as a financial safety net, shielding you from bearing the full financial burden of unexpected accidents or vehicle-related damages. Without insurance, these costs could be overwhelming and disrupt your financial stability.

Legal Requirement: In numerous states, having a minimum car insurance coverage is a legal requirement. Failing to meet these requirements can result in fines, license suspension, or legal consequences. It's essential to comply with your state's laws to avoid these consequences.

Peace of Mind: Car insurance offers peace of mind while driving. Knowing that you have coverage in place can alleviate stress and anxiety associated with the uncertainties of the road. This peace of mind allows you to focus on driving safely.

Understanding Types of Car Insurance Coverage

Car insurance consists of several types of coverage, each serving a specific purpose. When choosing coverage, ask questions to your insurance agency to understand which types are best for you:

Liability Coverage: This coverage pays for bodily injury and property damage to others in an accident where you are at fault. It is typically required by law. Ask about the minimum liability coverage your state mandates.

Collision Coverage: Collision coverage compensates for damage to your vehicle resulting from a collision, regardless of fault. Consider whether this coverage is necessary based on your vehicle's value and how prone you are to accidents.

Comprehensive Coverage: Comprehensive coverage covers non-collision-related damages, such as theft, vandalism, or natural disasters. It's essential to understand the deductibles and limits associated with comprehensive coverage.

Uninsured/Underinsured Motorist Coverage: This coverage protects you if you are involved in an accident with a driver with insufficient or no insurance. Ask about the coverage limits and whether it includes protection against hit-and-run accidents.

Medical Payments Coverage: Medical payment coverage helps pay for medical expenses incurred due to an accident, regardless of fault. Inquire about coverage limits and whether it includes passengers in your vehicle.

Personal Injury Protection (PIP): PIP covers medical expenses, lost wages, and other related costs for you and your passengers after an accident, regardless of fault. Ask about the scope of coverage and any additional benefits.

Selecting the Right Coverage

When choosing car insurance, assessing your needs and financial situation is crucial. Ask the following questions to determine the right coverage for you:

State Requirements: Understand your state's minimum insurance requirements, as they vary from state to state. Make sure you meet these requirements while considering additional coverage.

Budget: Determine how much you can comfortably spend on car insurance premiums while meeting your other financial obligations. Don't forget to ask about available discounts.

Vehicle Value: Consider the value of your vehicle. Older vehicles may not require as much coverage as new or high-value ones. Ask about the coverage options for different vehicle types.

Driving Habits: Evaluate your driving habits, such as daily commute distance, where you park your car, and the likelihood of accidents in your area. Ask about coverage options that suit your specific driving circumstances.

Additional Coverage: Assess whether additional coverages, like comprehensive or collision, are necessary based on your vehicle's value and the potential risks you face. Ask about the cost-benefit analysis of these coverages.

Deductibles: Choose deductibles that align with your budget and risk tolerance. A higher deductible typically results in lower premiums. Still, you'll pay more out of pocket in the event of a claim. Ask about deductible options and their impact on premiums.

In summary, car insurance is a legal requirement in many states and a critical financial safeguard. It's essential to understand the various types of coverage and ask questions to your insurance agency to select a plan tailored to your needs and budget. By doing so, you'll drive confidently, knowing you're protected in case of unexpected events.

Safety and Emergency Preparedness

Ensuring safety and being prepared for emergencies are paramount, especially for young adults transitioning to independent living. This comprehensive guide covers fire safety, emergency kits, evacuation plans, and staying safe during severe weather, with a focus on organization, clarity, and providing context to help you navigate potential challenges effectively:

Fire Safety and Prevention

Smoke Alarms: Your first line of defense against fires is a working smoke alarm. Install smoke alarms in critical areas of your residence, including bedrooms and common areas. Test them regularly and replace batteries as needed to ensure they function correctly. Smoke alarms are your early warning system in case of a fire.

Escape Routes: Take the time to familiarize yourself with your home's layout and identify multiple escape routes. Plan and practice evacuation drills, particularly if you share your living space with roommates. Having a clear escape plan is vital in high-stress situations.

Fire Extinguishers: Ensuring your safety and the safety of those around you is paramount. Have a fire safety plan in place, complete with designated meeting points and escape routes. Keep a fire extinguisher or fire blanket in an easily accessible location, and make sure you understand how to use it. Regularly check the extinguisher's expiration date to ensure it remains effective. Knowing how to operate these life-saving tools can make a significant difference during a small fire incident, providing you with peace of mind and the ability to respond swiftly and effectively if the need arises. Everyone in the house should know where the tools are and how to use them.

Cooking Safety: Practice safe cooking habits, such as staying in the kitchen while cooking, keeping flammable items away from heat sources, and turning off appliances when not in use. Cooking-related fires are among the most common residential fires, and prevention is key. This is where having a fire safety blanket nearby can save you and your home.

Creating an Emergency Kit

Vehicle Emergency Kit: When assembling your vehicle emergency kit, consider including solar-powered or hand-cranked tools that don't rely on batteries. These eco-friendly options can be invaluable in emergencies. If you live in an area prone to snowy conditions, don't forget to add a bag of kitty litter to your kit. It can provide traction if your vehicle gets stuck in snow or ice, helping you get back on the road safely. Your preparedness and resourcefulness will be your greatest allies during unexpected situations on the road.

Personal Needs: Tailor your emergency kit to your specific needs, including any required medications, hygiene products, and comfort items. Consider the unique needs of all household members, including pets.

Emergency Contacts: Include a list of emergency contacts in your kit, such as family members, friends, and local authorities, for quick reference during crises. Ensure everyone in your household knows how to use these contacts.

Regular Refresh: Periodically check and refresh your emergency kit, ensuring all items are in good condition and that food and water supplies have not expired. Make it a habit to review your kit at least once a year.

Evacuation Plans and Drills

Establish Meeting Points: Define specific meeting points outside your residence for evacuation. This ensures that everyone can be accounted for in case of an emergency. Share these meeting points with all household members.

Practice Evacuation Drills: Conduct regular evacuation drills, especially when sharing living space with others. Practice using various exit routes to enhance preparedness. Familiarity with evacuation routes reduces panic during emergencies.

Communication Plan: Develop a communication plan with roommates or neighbors to effectively relay vital information during an evacuation or emergency. Ensure that everyone knows how to contact each other in case of separation.

Know Community Resources: Familiarize yourself with local community resources, including emergency shelters and evacuation centers. This knowledge is essential if temporary relocation becomes necessary. Research and have a list of nearby emergency facilities.

Staying Safe in Severe Weather

Weather Alerts: Stay informed about weather conditions by utilizing weather apps, following local news, and subscribing to emergency alerts, ensuring you receive timely information. Being aware of changing weather patterns is crucial for proactive safety measures.

Emergency Weather Plans: Develop comprehensive plans for severe weather scenarios, such as storms, hurricanes, or tornadoes. Know where to take shelter and designate safe areas within your home. Create a "safe room" if needed.

Emergency Communication: Ensure that your phone remains charged and has alternative communication methods, such as a battery-powered radio, in case of power outages that disrupt regular communication channels. Reliable communication is vital during severe weather.

Emergency Contacts: Share emergency contacts with roommates or neighbors and establish a system for checking in on each other during severe weather events to enhance community safety. Working together can provide mutual support and assistance.

By prioritizing fire safety, creating a well-equipped emergency kit, practicing evacuation plans, and staying informed about severe weather, you can enhance your safety and that of others in your living space. These proactive measures empower you to respond effectively in emergencies, fostering a secure and prepared living environment. Remember, preparedness and knowledge are your best allies in times of crisis.

Key Takeaways

Financial Preparedness for Independent Living

- Assess your finances thoroughly, including income and expenses.
- Consider not only rent but also additional costs like utilities and groceries.
- Follow the 30% rule, spending no more than 30% of your income on rent.

Choosing the Right Location

- Select a location convenient for work or school to minimize commuting time and costs.
- Prioritize neighborhood safety and proximity to essential services and amenities.
- Consider your lifestyle preferences, such as urban or suburban living.

Apartment Hunting Tips

- Start your search early to have ample time for research.
- Utilize online platforms and attend open houses to find the right apartment.
- Create a checklist of essential features and ask the landlord questions.

Understanding Lease Agreements

- Carefully read and understand the lease agreement, including rent, duration, and maintenance clauses.
- Seek clarification on any ambiguous terms and understand security deposit details.
- Document the property's condition before moving in to protect your security deposit.

Ongoing Skills for Independent Living

▸ Independent living is an ongoing journey that involves managing your household, maintaining a clean living space, and fostering positive relationships with roommates.

▸ Regular decluttering, creating cleaning schedules, and sharing responsibilities with roommates are key to an organized and harmonious living environment.

▸ Basic home repair skills, emergency preparedness, and roommate communication contribute to a successful independent living experience.

Test Your Knowledge

1. When budgeting for rent, it's recommended not to spend more than what percentage of your monthly income?
   a. 40%
   b. 50%
   c. 30%
   d. 20%

2. What should you consider when choosing an apartment location?
   a. Proximity to shopping malls
   b. Proximity to work or school
   c. Noise level in the area
   d. Number of parks nearby

3. Before signing a lease agreement, it's essential to carefully read and understand all the _____ to avoid any surprises later.

4. Regular decluttering and creating a cleaning schedule helps in maintaining a _____ living space.

5. True or False: Emergency preparedness includes having a well-equipped emergency kit with essentials like non-perishable food and water.

CHAPTER 6

Technology and Online Life

I n the digital age, our lives have become increasingly intertwined with the online world. From socializing and shopping to studying and working, the internet plays a central role in our daily activities. While this connectivity offers incredible opportunities and convenience, it also brings about potential risks and challenges. This chapter is dedicated to helping you navigate the digital landscape safely and responsibly. We'll explore the importance of online security, responsible social media use, the significance of online privacy, and how to stay safe when engaging in online transactions. To drive home the significance of these topics, let's delve into the cautionary tale of Sean, a young individual who learned the hard way about the perils of neglecting online safety.

Sean's Cautionary Tale:

Meet Sean, a friendly and outgoing guy who loved exploring the online world. Sean had a diverse group of online friends, one of whom he had known for months through social media. They chatted regularly, sharing stories and experiences as if they'd known each other for years.

One day, Sean received a message from one of his friends on Snapchat, who claimed to be in a tight spot. They said they were stranded without gas money and needed help urgently. Trusting his friend, Sean didn't hesitate to offer assistance. He transferred the money without a second thought, thinking he was helping out a friend in need.

As the days passed, Sean realized he had fallen victim to a scam. He discovered that his friend's account had been hacked, and the person he had been helping was not his friend at all. This unfortunate experience left Sean feeling vulnerable and betrayed. He was thankful it was only $50 as it could have been much worse but it was a harsh lesson on the importance of online security and responsible online interactions. Through Sean's story, we'll explore how learning to protect yourself online can prevent similar hardships and ensure a safer and more enjoyable digital experience.

Digital Literacy and Online Security

Understanding Digital Literacy: In today's digital age, developing digital literacy means more than knowing how to use a computer; it's about navigating the complex online world with wisdom. It involves recognizing different file types, understanding common software applications, and honing critical thinking skills. Think of it as learning the rules of a vast digital game where critical thinking is your best strategy against misinformation.

Internet Safety: As you explore the online world, your safety should be a top concern. From recognizing malicious websites to understanding concepts like cookies and tracking, internet safety practices are like your shield against digital dangers. Knowing how to use secure Wi-Fi connections is akin to locking your virtual doors. Public Wi-Fi networks can be risky, just like leaving your front door wide open.

Media Literacy: In today's digital media era, being media literate is like having a pair of glasses that help you see through biases in news and content. It's also about distinguishing between credible and unreliable sources, like having a truth detector. Developing media literacy skills empowers you to navigate the vast online landscape with discernment.

Protecting Your Personal Information Online: Safeguarding your online presence is like safeguarding a treasure chest. Learning how to adjust privacy settings on social media platforms is your way of controlling who gets a glimpse of your treasures. Minimal sharing is a practice akin to not displaying all your treasures in public; avoid oversharing sensitive details like your address, phone number, or financial info. Using secure Wi-Fi connections is like sending your treasure chest via a secure courier. Being skeptical of requests for personal information is your shield against treasure hunters.

Recognizing Online Scams and Phishing: Familiarizing yourself with common phishing techniques is like learning to spot traps in an adventure game.

Verifying the legitimacy of emails and ensuring the security of websites you interact with are skills that protect you from falling into digital traps.

Password Best Practices: Think of passwords as keys to your digital castle. Creating complex and unique passwords is akin to having intricate locks on each door. Regularly changing passwords is like changing locks regularly. It's an extra layer of security to keep your castle safe.

Two-Factor Authentication

Enable Two-Factor Authentication (2FA): Two-Factor Authentication (2FA) is like having an extra lock on your treasure chest. It requires a second form of verification beyond your password, like a secret handshake. Enabling 2FA adds a critical layer of security to your online accounts.

Authentication Apps: While using text messages for 2FA is more secure than not having it at all, authentication apps take your security up a notch. They're like enchanted keys that work offline and can't be easily swiped by digital thieves.

Secure Backup: Think of backup codes as spare keys to your treasure chest. Safely storing these codes is crucial in case you lose your primary way of accessing your accounts.

Device Trustworthiness: Trustworthy devices are like trusted companions on your digital journey. Use them for secure access to your accounts, just like you'd trust a loyal friend. Avoid logging into sensitive accounts on untrusted devices to minimize the risk of unauthorized access.

Social Media Use and Online Etiquette

Responsible Social Media Posting: Think of your social media posts as messages in bottles. Consider the potential consequences before posting; once it's out there, it's hard to erase. Respecting others' privacy is essential for building and maintaining trust online. Promoting positivity is like being a beacon of light in a sea of negativity.

Interacting with Others on Social Media: Engage with empathy and active listening. It's like understanding different characters in a digital story.

Handling online disagreements maturely with credible sources and facts helps maintain productive dialogue.

Online Reputation Management: Think of your online reputation as your digital resume. Regularly curate your digital presence to reflect your growth and maturity. Consider how potential employers or colleagues might perceive your online image. Positive contributions to online communities, like sharing valuable content and engaging in meaningful discussions, make a difference in others' lives.

By adopting these practices, you'll navigate the digital landscape wisely and protect your online privacy and security effectively.

Purchasing and Meeting Online

For college-aged young adults venturing into online transactions, comprehending the intricacies of online shopping, arranging meetings with sellers or buyers, ensuring secure transactions, and adhering to online marketplace etiquette is paramount. Here is an extensive guide to help you navigate these aspects:

Online Shopping and Transaction Safety

Prioritize Secure Websites: Make secure websites with "https://" in the URL your first choice for online shopping. Stick to well-established online retailers known for their history of secure transactions.

Choose Trusted Platforms: Rely on trusted online shopping platforms. Platforms equipped with buyer protection mechanisms offer an additional layer of transaction security.

Opt for Secure Payment Methods: Select secure methods like credit cards or payment gateways with robust security features when making payments. Avoid transmitting sensitive information through unsecured channels.

Review Seller Ratings: Inspect seller reviews and ratings before making a purchase. Insights from previous buyers can help gauge the seller's reliability.

Ensuring Secure Transactions

Verify Product Details: Before completing a transaction, verify product details such as specifications, condition, and authenticity. Effective communication with the seller or buyer is essential.

Consider Escrow Services: For high-value transactions, contemplate using escrow services. These services hold funds until both parties fulfill their obligations, ensuring a secure transaction process.

Monitor Shipments: When purchasing items online, monitor the shipment's progress using the provided tracking numbers. Staying informed about the delivery status ensures a smooth process.

Understand Return Policies: Familiarize yourself with the return policies of online sellers. Understanding the return process can be crucial if the received item exceeds expectations.

Online Marketplace Etiquette

Maintain Clear Communication: Uphold clear and respectful communication with sellers or buyers. Address any queries or concerns before finalizing a transaction.

Timely Responses: Respond promptly to messages or inquiries. Timely communication fosters a positive buying or selling experience.

Provide Honest Descriptions: When selling items, furnish honest and accurate descriptions. Transparency builds trust between buyers and sellers.

Leave Feedback: After concluding a transaction, take a moment to leave feedback for the seller or buyer. Positive feedback acknowledges a smooth transaction, while constructive feedback can aid others in making informed decisions.

Meeting Sellers or Buyers in Person

If you're planning to meet someone whose ad you responded to in person, taking precautions is crucial to ensure your safety and a successful transaction. Here are some valuable tips:

Select Safe Meeting Spots

Public and Well-Lit Locations: Choose meeting places that are public, well-lit, and populated. Opt for venues with surveillance cameras and a steady flow of people. Consider places like shopping mall parking lots, coffee shops, or local police stations as meeting spots.

Daylight Hours: Whenever possible, schedule meetings during daylight hours. Daytime meetings offer better visibility and reduce potential risks associated with meeting at night.

Bring a Companion

Bringing a Friend: Whenever feasible, bring a friend or family member with you to the meeting. Having another person present provides an additional layer of security and can deter potential scammers or dishonest individuals.

Inform a Trusted Contact

Notify Someone: Before the meeting, inform a trusted friend or family member about your plans. Share essential details such as the meeting location, time, and the identity of the person you'll be meeting. Let them know when you expect to return.

Check-In: Arrange a check-in time with your trusted contact. After the meeting, contact them to confirm your safety and the successful completion of the transaction.

Trust Your Intuition

Listen to Your Gut: Trust your instincts during the meeting. If something doesn't feel right or seems uncomfortable, don't hesitate to take action. Your safety should always be the top priority.

Cancel or Relocate: If you have any doubts about the meeting or the other person's intentions, consider canceling the meeting or relocating it to a more public and secure setting. Your well-being is paramount.

Inspect Before Paying

Inspect the Product: Before making any payment, thoroughly inspect the product you intend to purchase. Ensure it meets your expectations and matches the description provided in the ad. Don't rush this process; take your time to examine the item carefully.

Payment Caution: Never pay for the product in advance or send money electronically without first inspecting the item in person. Scammers may ask for payment upfront and disappear once they receive the funds.

By following these guidelines when meeting sellers or buyers in person, you can minimize risks, protect your safety, and increase the likelihood of a successful and secure transaction. Remember that being cautious and prioritizing your well-being is essential when conducting in-person transactions with individuals you've met online.

You can securely navigate the digital marketplace by adhering to these guidelines for online shopping and transactions, arranging meetings with sellers or buyers, ensuring secure transactions, and practicing online marketplace etiquette. These practices contribute to a positive online commerce experience while minimizing potential risks.

Key Takeaways

Prioritize Online Security: Developing digital literacy and safeguarding personal information is crucial in the digital age. Take steps to protect your online presence, including setting strong passwords, enabling two-factor authentication, and being cautious about sharing personal information.

Practice Responsible Social Media Use: Social media plays a significant role in your online life. Think before you post, respect others' privacy, and engage in positive and constructive interactions. Your online reputation matters and can impact your personal and professional life.

Understand the Importance of Online Privacy: Your online privacy is essential for personal security. Be mindful of what you share online, adjust privacy settings on social media platforms, and practice secure browsing to minimize tracking and potential threats.

Stay Safe in Online Transactions: Whether you're shopping online or meeting someone for a transaction, prioritize safety. Choose secure websites, verify product details, and meet in well-lit, public locations when necessary. Responsible online marketplace etiquette can enhance your online commerce experience.

Continuously Educate Yourself: The digital landscape is constantly evolving. Stay informed about online privacy issues, emerging threats, and best practices. By staying educated, you empower yourself to navigate the digital world safely and responsibly.

Test Your Knowledge

1. What does HTTPS in a website URL indicate?
   a. High-speed Internet connection
   b. Highly Secure Encryption Protocol
   c. Hyperlinked Text and Secure Pages
   d. High-Efficiency Transaction Service
2. Which of the following is NOT a recommended practice for online privacy?
   a. Using a Virtual Private Network (VPN)
   b. Regularly reviewing and customizing privacy settings on social media.
   c. Conducting sensitive transactions on public Wi-Fi networks
   d. Adjusting browser privacy settings to minimize tracking
3. What is the purpose of Two-Factor Authentication (2FA)?
   a. It requires two separate internet connections for added security.
   b. It verifies your identity with a fingerprint and a passcode.
   c. It adds an extra layer of security by requiring a second form of verification.
   d. It encrypts all your online communications.
4. When meeting sellers or buyers in person for transactions, it's important to choose _____, well-lit, and public locations.
5. Leaving constrvs. (True/False)

CHAPTER 7

Mental Health and Well-Being

Picture this: Boston, a young adult with a zest for life, decided to take the plunge and move to a new city in pursuit of an exciting job opportunity. Leaving behind the comfort of home, old friends, and the ever-supportive embrace of family, Boston was ready to embrace independence and kickstart a new chapter.

But as the initial thrill of adventure settled, the reality of being on his own started to sink in. Friends were miles away, and adulting came with a whole bunch of responsibilities he hadn't quite prepared for. What was once a thrilling escapade quickly turned into a battle against feelings of isolation and overwhelm, threatening to overshadow his journey.

And then, there was work. Boston's newfound struggles weren't going unnoticed. A perceptive colleague named Michael spotted the change in him. Instead of brushing it off, Michael decided to lend a helping hand. It might have seemed like a small gesture, but it made a world of difference.

Through heartfelt conversations and shared experiences, Boston learned the power of opening up about his struggles. He discovered that it's okay to ask for help and that vulnerability can be a strength. With the support of friends like Alex, Boston not only salvaged his job but embarked on a journey of self-discovery and emotional growth.

Now, as we dive into this chapter, we're entering the world of mental health and well-being, a place where stories like Boston's are part of the journey. Here, we'll explore the fundamental principles that underlie your emotional and mental health during this transformative phase of life.

This chapter will equip you with the tools to protect your mental well-being, help you recognize when it's time to seek assistance, and lay the groundwork for emotional resilience. We'll delve into strategies for personal growth, nurturing positive relationships, and providing you with the resources needed to navigate the complexities of young adulthood.

Your mental well-being is like a compass, guiding you through uncharted waters and helping you carve a path to lasting success and a life filled with fulfillment. Welcome to the world of mental health and well-being, where you hold the pen to craft your own story of growth and resilience.

What Is Mental Health?

It's not just a fancy term; it's all about how you're doing on the inside – emotionally, mentally, and socially. Think of it as the backstage pass to your life, influencing how you handle stress, connect with others, and make those everyday decisions. But here's the deal: it's not just about dodging mental disorders; it's about rocking life's ups and downs, building awesome relationships, and staying on top of your game.

The Importance of Mental Health

Holistic Well-Being: Holistic well-being emphasizes the interconnectedness of various aspects of your health. Mental health is a fundamental pillar in this framework, as it closely interacts with physical health and emotional stability. When nurtured, it contributes to an integrated sense of wellness that harmonizes these elements, fostering a balanced and healthy state of being.

Quality of Life: The influence of mental health on your quality of life cannot be overstated. A well-maintained mental state enriches your existence with a profound sense of purpose, satisfaction, and the capacity to derive meaning from every facet of life, both mundane and exceptional.

Coping with Stress: Mental well-being equips you with an array of effective stress-coping mechanisms. These tools enhance your capacity to withstand and adapt to life's inevitable challenges. By promoting resilience and adaptability, good mental health fortifies you against the adverse effects of stress.

Productivity and Success: Mental health is an invaluable asset on your journey to academic and professional success. It plays a pivotal role in sharpening cognitive faculties, enhancing decision-making abilities, and propelling you toward your personal and career goals. A well-maintained mental state provides the clarity and determination needed to achieve success.

Interpersonal Relationships: The impact of mental health extends to your interpersonal relationships. It molds your ability to communicate effectively, empathize with others, and cultivate meaningful connections. A strong foundation in mental health can greatly enhance the quality and depth of your relationships.

Emotional Regulation: Proficiency in emotional regulation is a core aspect of mental health. It empowers you to comprehend and manage your emotions in a constructive and adaptive manner. This skill ensures that you can navigate the spectrum of human feelings while maintaining emotional equilibrium.

Reducing Stigma: Prioritizing mental health initiatives is instrumental in combating the persistent stigma surrounding mental health issues. Initiating open and honest dialogues, coupled with widespread awareness campaigns, plays a pivotal role in fostering a more compassionate and understanding society. By reducing stigma, we pave the way for individuals to seek and receive the support they need without fear or discrimination.

Common Mental Health Challenges

Anxiety Disorders: Anxiety disorders indeed encompass various types, as mentioned earlier. In addition to generalized anxiety disorder, panic disorder, and social anxiety disorder, it's worth noting other types such as specific phobias (intense fears of specific objects or situations) and obsessive-compulsive disorder (characterized by persistent, intrusive thoughts and repetitive behaviors).

Depression: Depression is indeed a significant mood disorder. It's essential to emphasize that there are different forms of depression, including major depressive disorder (characterized by persistent sadness and a loss of interest or pleasure in activities), seasonal affective disorder (depression that occurs at specific times of the year, often in the winter), and persistent depressive disorder (a long-lasting form of depression).

Stress-Related Disorders: Chronic stress can indeed lead to various physical and mental health challenges. It's important to mention that stress-related disorders can also include adjustment disorders (excessive stress or difficulty coping with significant life changes), acute stress disorder (resulting from exposure to a traumatic event), and complex PTSD (a more severe form of PTSD often stemming from prolonged trauma or multiple traumatic events).

Eating Disorders: In addition to anorexia nervosa, bulimia nervosa, and binge-eating disorder, there are other eating disorders to be aware of, such as avoidant/restrictive food intake disorder (ARFID), which involves limited food preferences and aversions, and orthorexia nervosa, characterized by an obsession with healthy eating.

Substance Use Disorders: Alongside substance abuse, it's essential to mention substance dependence, which involves physical and psychological reliance on a substance, as well as co-occurring disorders (individuals who experience both a mental health disorder and a substance use disorder simultaneously).

Attention-Deficit/Hyperactivity Disorder (ADHD): In addition to academic and occupational performance, ADHD can also impact relationships and daily functioning. It's valuable to know that there are three types of ADHD: primarily inattentive presentation (predominantly difficulties with attention), primarily hyperactive-impulsive presentation (predominantly hyperactivity and impulsivity), and combined presentation (a mix of inattention, hyperactivity, and impulsivity).

Bipolar Disorder: Bipolar disorder is characterized by extreme mood swings, including manic episodes (elevated mood, increased energy, and impulsivity) and depressive episodes (profound sadness and loss of interest). Understanding the nuances of this disorder can help individuals manage it effectively.

Schizophrenia: Schizophrenia is a severe mental disorder that affects thinking, emotions, and behavior. Symptoms may include hallucinations, delusions, disorganized thinking, and impaired social functioning.

Recognizing Mental Health Warning Signs

Changes in Behavior: Be alert to noticeable shifts in behavior, such as increasing isolation, withdrawing from social activities, or showing a sudden decline in interests and hobbies. These changes may indicate underlying mental health concerns.

Mood Swings: Extreme mood swings, persistent feelings of sadness, irritability, or heightened anxiety that significantly impact daily functioning should be noted. These mood fluctuations may suggest the need for mental health support.

Sleep Disturbances: Pay attention to significant changes in sleep patterns, including persistent insomnia or excessive sleeping. Sleep disruptions can often be early indicators of emotional distress.

Appetite Changes: Noticeable shifts in appetite leading to significant weight loss or gain should be observed. Changes in eating habits can be linked to emotional well-being.

Energy Levels: Persistent fatigue, low energy levels, or a lack of motivation that hinders regular activities can be indicative of underlying mental health challenges.

Cognitive Challenges: Be aware of difficulties in concentration, decision-making, or experiencing memory lapses. Cognitive challenges may signal emotional distress and should not be overlooked.

Physical Symptoms: Unexplained physical symptoms like frequent headaches, stomachaches, or unexplained bodily pains should be taken seriously, as they can be linked to mental health issues.

Self-Harm or Risky Behavior: Be vigilant about signs of self-harming behaviors or engaging in risky activities without consideration for consequences. These actions may be expressions of emotional turmoil.

Identifying Signs of Mental Health Struggles

Social Withdrawal: Recognize when individuals avoid social interactions, isolate themselves from friends, family, or regular activities. Social withdrawal can be a red flag for mental health struggles.

Expressing Hopelessness: Pay attention when someone verbalizes feelings of hopelessness, worthlessness, or expresses a belief that life is not worth living. These expressions may indicate severe emotional distress.

Changes in Academic Performance: Be attuned to significant declines in academic performance or signs of disengagement from educational pursuits. Academic changes can often reflect underlying mental health challenges.

Substance Use: Notice any escalation in substance use as a coping mechanism for mental health struggles. Self-medication through substances can indicate underlying emotional difficulties.

Increased Anxiety: Acknowledge heightened anxiety levels, panic attacks, or an inability to manage stress. Increased anxiety may be a sign that someone is struggling emotionally.

Neglecting Self-Care: Observe when individuals neglect personal hygiene, appearance, or self-care routines. Lack of self-care can be linked to mental health issues.

Lack of Interest: Take note when someone loses interest in activities they once enjoyed or displays a decreased passion for their hobbies. A decline in enthusiasm may indicate emotional challenges.

How to Approach Someone in Need

Express Concern: Approach the person with empathy, expressing genuine concern for their well-being. Let them know you care and are there to support them.

Listen Actively: Provide a non-judgmental and compassionate space for them to express their feelings. Active listening is crucial for creating a safe environment.

Ask Direct Questions: If appropriate, ask direct but caring questions about their mental health. For example, say, "I've noticed some changes; how are you feeling?" This shows you're open to discussing their emotions.

Offer Assistance: Extend your support and assistance in seeking professional help through counseling services, therapy, or mental health resources. Be proactive in helping them access the necessary support.

Encourage Professional Help: Encourage them to reach out to mental health professionals for guidance and support. Highlight the importance of seeking expert assistance when facing emotional difficulties.

Reducing Mental Health Stigma

Education and Awareness: Promote education and awareness about mental health to dispel myths and misconceptions. Understanding mental health is a crucial step in reducing stigma.

Open Conversations: Foster open conversations about mental health, creating a supportive environment where individuals feel comfortable sharing their experiences and seeking help when needed.

Share Personal Stories: Share personal stories of overcoming mental health challenges to inspire hope and reduce stigma. Sharing experiences can help others feel less alone in their struggles.

Language Matters: Be mindful of the language used when discussing mental health. Use respectful, inclusive, and non-stigmatizing language that fosters understanding and compassion.

Supportive Communities: Work towards building supportive communities where individuals feel safe seeking help without fear of judgment. Community support is essential for breaking down stigma barriers.

By recognizing these mental health warning signs, identifying signs of mental health struggles, approaching individuals with care and support, and actively working to reduce mental health stigma, we can collectively contribute to a culture of empathy, understanding, and unwavering support. Creating an environment where mental health is openly discussed and prioritized is instrumental in building resilient and compassionate communities.

Effective Coping Mechanisms

Mindfulness Meditation: Embrace mindfulness meditation to stay present and nurture a non-judgmental awareness of your thoughts and emotions. Meditation isn't just about relaxation; it's about enhancing focus and taming stress. Consider using mindfulness apps or guided meditation sessions to get started.

Deep Breathing Exercises: Incorporate deep breathing exercises into your daily routine to tackle stress and anxiety head-on. Controlled breathing acts as a calming agent, contributing to your overall well-being. You can find various breathing techniques online or through mobile apps.

Physical Activity: Regular physical activity is your ally in this journey. Exercise releases endorphins, your body's natural mood elevators, promoting physical and mental health. Find an activity you enjoy, whether it's jogging, dancing, or yoga, and make it a part of your routine.

Journaling: Grab a journal and pour your thoughts and feelings into it. Writing can be therapeutic, helping you process emotions, gain clarity, and sometimes discover new facets of yourself. Consider daily journaling prompts to kickstart your writing practice.

Social Connections: Nurture your social connections. Spending quality time with friends and loved ones provides emotional support and a profound sense of belonging. Reach out to friends for regular catch-ups, and make an effort to strengthen your social bonds.

Positive Affirmations: Empower yourself with positive affirmations. These little mantras can challenge and reshape negative self-talk, boosting self-esteem and fostering a positive mindset. Create a list of affirmations that resonate with you and recite them daily.

Artistic Expression: Dive into creative outlets like art, music, or writing. Expressing yourself creatively can be a powerful way to navigate the turbulent sea of emotions. You don't need to be a professional artist; the act of creating itself can be therapeutic.

The Role of Self-Care

Prioritize Rest: Give yourself the gift of sufficient sleep. Quality sleep is a cornerstone of cognitive function, mood regulation, and well-being. Establish a consistent sleep schedule and create a bedtime routine that promotes relaxation.

Healthy Nutrition: What you eat directly affects your physical and mental health. Opt for a balanced and nutritious diet to fuel your journey to well-being. Include a variety of fruits, vegetables, lean proteins, and whole grains in your meals.

Establish Boundaries: Learn to set and maintain healthy boundaries in your relationships and work. These boundaries are not just limits but shields guarding your well-being. Communicate your boundaries clearly to those around you.

Time Management: Master the art of time management. Prioritize tasks, set achievable goals, and ensure you allocate time for both work and leisure. Consider using time management techniques like the Pomodoro Technique or task prioritization methods.

Digital Detox: Unplug from screens periodically. Constant digital exposure can contribute to stress and impact your mental health. Give yourself the gift of a digital detox by designating tech-free hours or days to recharge.

Pamper Yourself: Make self-pampering a ritual. Whether indulging in a relaxing bath, losing yourself in a favorite hobby, or taking a leisurely walk, prioritize activities that bring you joy. Schedule regular "me-time" to recharge your spirit.

Learn to Say No: Practice the art of saying no when necessary. Overcommitting can lead to burnout. Prioritize your well-being by managing your commitments wisely. Remember that saying no to one thing often means saying yes to yourself.

Developing Your Self-Care Routine

Self-Reflection: Reflect on activities that bring you peace and joy. Identify those who contribute to your well-being, and let them become your daily companions. Consider journaling your self-reflections to track your progress.

Consistency is Key: Establish a routine that incorporates self-care activities. Consistency fosters a habit of making your well-being a top priority. Create a daily or weekly self-care schedule that fits seamlessly into your life.

Experiment with Activities: Venture into various self-care activities. Explore the vast world of possibilities, from reading and nature walks to simple moments of quiet reflection. Keep an open mind and experiment with different practices to discover what resonates with you.

Adjust as Needed: Be adaptable with your self-care routine. Life is a dynamic journey, and your self-care toolkit may need adjustments to accommodate changing circumstances. Regularly assess your needs and tweak your routine accordingly to ensure it continues to serve you well.

Stress Management

Identifying Stress and Effective Strategies

Identify Stressors: Acknowledge the sources of stress in your life. Recognizing stressors is the first step in taming them effectively. Keep a journal to track what triggers your stress, helping you gain insight into recurring patterns.

Time Management Techniques: Use time management techniques to organize tasks and prevent feeling overwhelmed. Divide large tasks into smaller, more manageable steps. Consider using time management tools or apps to help structure your day.

Mind-Body Techniques: Embrace mind-body practices like yoga or tai chi. These activities combine physical movement with mindfulness, fostering relaxation. Attend classes or watch online tutorials to get started.

Seek Support: Contact friends, family, or mental health professionals. Sharing your stressors can provide valuable insights and emotional relief. Reach out to support groups or therapists specializing in stress management.

Set Realistic Expectations: Establish attainable expectations for yourself. Perfectionism can be a silent stressor. Embrace a mindset of progress, not perfection, and set achievable goals for yourself.

Humor and Laughter: Inject humor into your life. Laughter is a natural stress reliever that can elevate your mood, even during challenging times. Watch comedies, read funny books, or spend time with people who make you laugh.

Understanding Stress

What Is Stress?: Stress is your body's built-in response to demands and threats. It gears you up to confront or avoid perceived danger. Stress is a part of life, but chronic or excessive stress can adversely affect your physical and mental health.

The Two Types of Stress:

- **Acute Stress:** This is short-term stress triggered by immediate challenges. It's a normal part of life, often motivating quick action. Examples include preparing for a presentation or dealing with a sudden deadline.
- **Chronic Stress:** This is persistent, long-term stress resulting from ongoing pressure, such as work, finances, or relationships. If left unmanaged, chronic stress can harm your health and well-being.

Daily Stress Management Techniques

Time Management: Prioritize tasks and set realistic goals. Breaking tasks into smaller, manageable steps can reduce feelings of overwhelm. Use techniques like the Eisenhower Matrix to prioritize effectively.

Mindfulness and Deep Breathing: Practice mindfulness exercises and techniques to remain calm and composed when faced with daily stressors. Deep breathing exercises, like the 4-7-8 technique, can help you stay grounded.

Physical Activity: Incorporate regular physical activity into your daily life. Exercise reduces stress and contributes to your overall physical and mental well-being. Find an activity you enjoy, whether it's jogging, dancing, or yoga, and make it a part of your routine.

Healthy Nutrition: Maintain a balanced diet with nourishing foods. Proper nutrition supports your well-being and equips your body to handle stress.

Focus on consuming a variety of fruits, vegetables, lean proteins, and whole grains.

Social Connections: Cultivate positive social connections. Spending time with friends and loved ones provides emotional support and reduces feelings of isolation. Plan regular gatherings or virtual meet-ups with loved ones.

Establishing Boundaries: Master setting boundaries in your relationships and work. Understanding your limits and communicating them effectively can prevent unnecessary stress. Learn to say "no" when you need to without feeling guilty.

Mindful Breaks: Take short breaks to engage in joyful or relaxed activities during your day. Even a few minutes of mindful breaks can make a significant difference. Practice mini-meditations or go for a short walk to clear your mind.

Strategies for Long-Term Stress Reduction

Regular Exercise Routine: Develop a consistent exercise routine. Physical activity reduces stress and enhances your overall well-being. Aim for at least 150 minutes of moderate-intensity exercise per week.

Mindfulness Practices: Engage in mindfulness practices such as meditation or yoga. These practices cultivate a calm and focused mind, reducing the impact of chronic stress. Start with guided meditation apps or beginner-friendly yoga classes.

Counseling and Therapy: Consider seeking professional counseling or therapy. Speaking with a mental health professional can provide valuable insights and effective coping strategies. Therapy sessions can be conducted in person or online for convenience.

Time for Hobbies: Dedicate time to activities you enjoy. Hobbies and leisure pursuits offer a healthy escape from daily stressors. Whether it's painting, playing a musical instrument, or gardening, prioritize activities that bring you joy.

Healthy Sleep Patterns: Establish and maintain healthy sleep patterns. Quality sleep is crucial for stress management and your overall well-being.

Create a comfortable sleep environment and stick to a consistent sleep schedule.

Stress-Reducing Techniques: Learn and practice progressive muscle relaxation, guided imagery, or biofeedback techniques to enhance stress management skills. These techniques can help you manage stress in real-time.

Positive Lifestyle Changes: Make positive lifestyle changes, such as reducing caffeine intake, quitting smoking, or moderating alcohol consumption. These changes contribute to a healthier stress response and overall well-being.

Problem-Solving Skills: Hone your problem-solving skills. Effective strategies for approaching and resolving challenges can significantly reduce the impact of stressors. Consider reading books or taking courses on problem-solving techniques.

Taking a Holistic Approach to Stress Management

Self-Reflection: Regularly reflect on your stressors and how you respond to them. Understanding your triggers is a pivotal step in effective stress management. Journal your reflections to gain deeper insights.

Seeking Support: Don't hesitate to seek support from friends, family, or support groups. Sharing your feelings and experiences can provide valuable emotional relief. Join online or local support groups to connect with others facing similar challenges.

Flexibility and Adaptability: Cultivate flexibility and adaptability in the face of change. Accept that some stressors are beyond your control, and this acceptance can significantly reduce feelings of helplessness. Practice mindfulness to stay present and adaptable.

Positive Outlook: Foster a positive outlook on life. Cultivate gratitude and focus on aspects of life that bring you joy and fulfillment. Maintain a gratitude journal to regularly remind yourself of the positive aspects of your life.

Seeking Professional Help

When to Consider Professional Help

Persistent Distress: If feelings of distress persist and interfere with your daily life, it may be time to seek professional help. It's essential to recognize that seeking help is a proactive step toward better mental health. Therapists are trained to assist individuals in managing and alleviating distressing emotions.

Impact on Functioning: When emotional struggles start affecting your relationships, work, or academic performance, professional intervention can be beneficial. Mental health professionals can help you develop coping strategies and provide support to regain control over your life.

Changes in Behavior: Significant changes in behavior, such as withdrawal, excessive anger, or risky actions, may indicate the need for professional support. These behavioral changes can be signs of underlying emotional or psychological issues that require attention and guidance.

Intense Emotions: Experiencing intense and overwhelming emotions, such as anxiety or sadness, that are difficult to manage on your own can be a clear signal to seek professional help. Therapists can teach you techniques to regulate your emotions effectively.

Trauma or Loss: Coping with trauma, grief, or significant life changes may necessitate the guidance of a mental health professional. Traumatic experiences and grief can have a profound impact on mental well-being, and therapy can provide a structured and supportive environment for healing.

Substance Use Issues: If substance use becomes problematic and begins to impact various aspects of your life, seeking professional help is crucial. Substance abuse often co-occurs with underlying mental health issues, and addressing both simultaneously is essential for recovery.

How to Find and Choose a Therapist

Referrals: Seek recommendations from friends, family, or primary care providers. Personal referrals often provide valuable insights into the therapist's effectiveness and compatibility.

Online Directories: Utilize online directories to find therapists in your area. Websites like Psychology Today or therapy-specific directories can be useful for browsing profiles and specialties.

Insurance Providers: Check with your insurance provider to identify therapists covered by your plan. This ensures financial feasibility and minimizes out-of-pocket expenses.

Professional Organizations: Explore professional organizations such as the American Psychological Association (APA) for lists of qualified therapists. Membership in such organizations often signifies a commitment to ethical standards and continuing education.

Initial Consultations: Schedule initial consultations with potential therapists to assess their approach, expertise, and whether you feel comfortable working with them. This introductory meeting allows you to ask questions and discuss your specific needs.

Understanding the Therapy Process - What to Expect

Confidentiality: Therapists adhere to strict confidentiality guidelines, creating a safe, open, and honest communication space. They can only breach confidentiality in specific situations, such as if there is a risk of harm to yourself or others.

Collaborative Relationship: Therapy involves a collaborative relationship between the client and therapist. Working together towards defined goals is a key aspect. Your therapist should respect your input and actively involve you in your treatment plan.

Goal Setting: Establish clear goals with your therapist. Whether addressing specific issues or personal growth, setting goals provides direction and helps you track your progress throughout therapy.

Evidence-Based Approaches: Therapists use evidence-based approaches tailored to individual needs. Common modalities include cognitive-behavioral therapy (CBT) or dialectical behavior therapy (DBT). These approaches have been extensively researched and proven effective for various mental health challenges.

Regular Sessions: Therapy typically involves regular sessions, with the frequency determined by individual needs and therapeutic goals. Consistency is essential for achieving lasting results, and your therapist will help you determine the appropriate schedule.

Homework and Reflection: Therapists may assign homework or encourage reflection between sessions to enhance the therapeutic process. These tasks can help you practice and apply the skills and strategies learned in therapy to real-life situations.

Online Mental Health Resources: A Guide for You

Accessing Reliable Mental Health Information

Educational Websites: Explore reputable websites like the National Institute of Mental Health (NIMH) or mental health sections of respected health organizations for reliable information. These websites often provide comprehensive resources on various mental health topics.

University Resources: Check if your college or university offers mental health resources online. Many educational institutions provide information and support services for students, including access to counseling and crisis hotlines.

Online Libraries and Articles: Utilize online libraries and academic articles to access scholarly information related to mental health. Academic databases often provide in-depth insights into the latest research and treatments.

Psychology and Mental Health Apps: Consider using reputable mental health apps that provide information, self-help tools, and resources. Ensure trusted organizations develop these apps, and read user reviews to gauge their effectiveness and user-friendliness. These apps can complement professional treatment and assist in managing mental health challenges.

Online Support Communities

Social Media Groups: Join mental health support groups on social media platforms. These groups provide a space for sharing experiences, seeking advice, and connecting with others facing similar challenges.

Online Forums: Explore dedicated mental health forums and communities where you can anonymously discuss your experiences, offer support, and share coping strategies.

University Forums and Groups:

- Check if your college or university has online forums or groups where students can discuss mental health.
- Share resources.
- Offer support to one another.

Community-Based Platforms: Participate in community-based mental health platforms focusing on specific topics or concerns. These platforms often include expert moderators to ensure a supportive environment.

Teletherapy and Online Counseling

Teletherapy Platforms: Explore teletherapy platforms that connect you with licensed therapists for virtual counseling sessions. Ensure these platforms prioritize user privacy and adhere to ethical standards.

University Counseling Services: Check if your college or university offers online counseling services. Many educational institutions provide virtual counseling sessions to support students' mental health.

Mental Health Hotlines: Access online mental health hotlines that offer immediate support and resources. These services can be crucial during times of crisis or when in need of urgent assistance.

Tailoring Online Mental Health Resources for You

Digital Literacy: Emphasize the importance of digital literacy when navigating online mental health resources. Learn how to evaluate the credibility of information and recognize reputable sources.

Cultural Sensitivity: Highlight the significance of seeking mental health information that is culturally sensitive and inclusive. Explore resources that respect and reflect diverse backgrounds.

Privacy and Security: Emphasize the importance of choosing secure and privacy-focused platforms, especially when engaging in online support communities or teletherapy. Prioritize your privacy for a safe online experience.

Balanced Use: Remember to maintain a balanced use of online mental health resources. While these tools can be valuable, it's essential to complement them with in-person support and professional guidance when needed.

Following this guide can enhance your well-being in the digital age. Emphasizing the importance of cultural sensitivity, digital literacy, and privacy ensures a tailored and holistic approach to your mental health support.

Being There for Friends and Loved Ones

Online Support Communities

Social Media Groups: Join mental health support groups on social media platforms like Facebook or Reddit. These groups provide a space for sharing experiences, seeking advice, and connecting with others facing similar challenges. Remember to be cautious with sharing personal information and choose groups moderated by responsible individuals.

Online Forums: Explore dedicated mental health forums and communities where you can anonymously discuss your experiences, offer support, and share coping strategies. Websites like Reddit have specific subreddits dedicated to mental health discussions, creating a supportive environment for users.

University Forums and Groups: Check if your college or university has online forums or groups where students can discuss mental health. These forums can be valuable for sharing resources, offering support to one another, and finding comfort in knowing that others in your academic community may be going through similar experiences.

Community-Based Platforms: Participate in community-based mental health platforms focusing on specific topics or concerns, such as anxiety, depression, or LGBTQ+ issues. These platforms often include expert moderators to ensure a supportive environment and provide valuable insights from professionals.

Teletherapy and Online Counseling

Teletherapy Platforms: Explore teletherapy platforms that connect you with licensed therapists for virtual counseling sessions. Ensure these platforms prioritize user privacy and adhere to ethical standards. Teletherapy can offer a convenient way to access professional mental health support from the comfort of your home.

University Counseling Services: Check if your college or university offers online counseling services. Many educational institutions provide virtual counseling sessions to support students' mental health. These services are often tailored to the unique challenges that students face.

Mental Health Hotlines: Access online mental health hotlines that offer immediate support and resources. These services can be crucial during times of crisis or when in need of urgent assistance. Examples include crisis text lines or online chat support services.

Tailoring Online Mental Health Resources for You

Digital Literacy: Emphasize the importance of digital literacy when navigating online mental health resources. Learn how to evaluate the credibility of information and recognize reputable sources. Look for websites or resources that cite scientific research and are reviewed by mental health professionals.

Cultural Sensitivity: Highlight the significance of seeking mental health information that is culturally sensitive and inclusive. Explore resources that respect and reflect diverse backgrounds. Culturally competent mental health resources can provide more relevant and effective support.

Privacy and Security: Emphasize the importance of choosing secure and privacy-focused platforms, especially when engaging in online support communities or teletherapy. Prioritize your privacy for a safe online experience by using platforms that encrypt your data and have clear privacy policies.

Balanced Use: Remember to maintain a balanced use of online mental health resources. While these tools can be valuable, it's essential to complement them with in-person support and professional guidance when needed. Online resources can be a supplement to traditional mental health care, not a replacement.

By following this tips, you can enhance your well-being in the digital age. Emphasizing the importance of cultural sensitivity, digital literacy, and privacy ensures a tailored and holistic approach to your mental health support, empowering you to make informed decisions about your well-being.

Being There for Friends and Loved Ones

Providing Emotional Support

Active Listening: Practice active listening when friends or loved ones share their struggles. This involves giving them your full attention, asking open-ended questions, and reflecting on their feelings. Validating their emotions and expressing empathy can make them feel heard and understood.

Avoid Judgment: Refrain from passing judgment or offering unsolicited advice. Creating a non-judgmental space encourages open communication, where individuals feel safe sharing their thoughts and emotions without fear of criticism.

Express Concern: Express genuine concern for their well-being. Let them know you care about their happiness and mental health. Simple gestures like checking in on them regularly or sending a caring message can make a significant difference.

Encourage Openness: Encourage openness about seeking professional help. Normalize the idea that therapy is a positive and proactive step toward better mental health. Share information about available resources and offer to assist them in finding a suitable therapist if needed. Your support can be instrumental in their journey to recovery and well-being.

Key Takeaways

Prioritize Your Mental Health: Mental health is an integral part of overall well-being, influencing your emotions, behaviors, and decisions. Take proactive steps to safeguard your mental health, just as you would with your physical health.

Recognize Signs and Seek Help: Be aware of common mental health challenges like anxiety, depression, and stress-related disorders. If you experience persistent distress, significant behavior changes, or intense emotions that interfere with daily life, consider seeking professional help.

Utilize Online and Offline Resources: Leverage online mental health resources, such as support communities, forums, and teletherapy, for information and support. Maintain a balance between online and offline support, complementing digital resources with in-person connections and professional guidance.

Support Others Compassionately: Learn to provide emotional support to friends and loved ones who may be facing mental health challenges. Practice active listening, express empathy, and encourage open conversations about seeking professional help.

Test Your Knowledge

1. Which of the following is NOT a common symptom of anxiety disorders?
    a. Excessive worry and fear
    b. Rapid heartbeat
    c. Persistent sadness
    d. Muscle tension
2. Depression is often characterized by _____.
    a. Extreme happiness and euphoria
    b. A persistent feeling of sadness and hopelessness

      c.   Frequent mood swings

      d.   Overly high self-esteem

3.   What is one effective way to manage stress and promote mental well-being?

      a.   Isolating yourself from others

      b.   Avoiding all forms of physical activity

      c.   Practicing relaxation techniques like deep breathing and meditation

      d.   Consuming large amounts of caffeine

4.   A strong support network of friends and family can provide valuable _____ during difficult times.

5.   Mental health is just as important as _____ health, and both should be prioritized for overall well-being.

CHAPTER 8

Managing Important Documents and Financial Security

Importance of Vital Documents:

▸ Vital documents, such as birth certificates, social security cards, passports, and IDs, are the foundation of your identity and financial stability.

Effective Document Management

▸ Organized document management offers numerous benefits, including quick responses to life events, financial security, health and emergency preparedness, legal compliance, and reduced stress.

Birth Certificate and Its Significance

▸ Birth certificates confirm your identity and citizenship in various official transactions.
▸ It is vital in accessing essential services, proving your citizenship status, and verifying your identity when needed.
▸ Safeguard it through secure storage, copies with trusted family members, and digital backup.
▸ Replacement procedures are available if it's lost, involving contacting vital records, verifying your identity, and following government agency instructions.

Social Security Card

- Your Social Security Number (SSN) is essential for various government-related transactions.
- Employers use it for income reporting and payroll, lenders for credit history, and government programs like Social Security, Medicare, and welfare.
- Protect your SSN by minimizing sharing, ensuring data security, and being cautious of scams.
- Replacement procedures are available for lost or stolen SSN cards, which involve reporting the loss to the Social Security Administration, completing an application form, and providing necessary documentation.

Passports and Travel Documents

- Passports are essential for international travel and identification.
- Plan and confirm your eligibility before applying for a passport.
- Gather essential paperwork, including a completed application form, a copy of your birth certificate or previous passport, and a government-issued photo ID.
- Obtain passport-sized photos meeting specified criteria.
- Report and replace lost or stolen passports promptly to your local authorities and the country's consulate or embassy.

Personal Identification Cards

- Understanding the process of obtaining a driver's license or ID is crucial.
- Review eligibility criteria, gather required documents, and prepare for exams if applicable.
- Visit the Department of Motor Vehicles (DMV) to submit your application, provide necessary documentation, and possibly take examinations.

▸ Ensure you have a valid form of personal identification and know the replacement process if it's lost, including reporting the loss to the police, visiting the DMV for a replacement, and covering associated fees.

Financial and Legal Paperwork

▸ Manage income tax documents diligently, understand your insurance policies, and prioritize password security in the digital age.
▸ Implement secure storage methods for crucial physical and digital documents.
▸ Regularly review and assess insurance plans to ensure they align with your evolving needs and make adjustments as necessary due to life changes.

Key Takeaways:

Safeguard Vital Documents: Protecting birth certificates, Social Security cards, passports, and IDs is crucial. Safely store physical copies, share copies with trusted family members, and maintain digital backups to ensure you can access essential services and prove your identity when needed.

Stay Informed and Prepared: Understand the processes for obtaining and replacing vital documents, such as birth certificates, Social Security cards, passports, and IDs. Additionally, prioritize secure document management, whether physical or digital, to navigate life's challenges confidently and maintain your financial and personal well-being.

Test Your Knowledge

1. What is the primary purpose of a birth certificate?
   a. To prove your eligibility for government benefits
   b. To confirm your identity and citizenship
   c. To access financial services
   d. To apply for a driver's license

2. What should you do if you lose your Social Security card?
   a. Report it to the local police
   b. Wait for it to turn up on its
   c. Contact the Social Security Admin and follow their replacement process
   d. Use a copy of your birth certificate as a replacement
3. Why is maintaining a digital backup of your passport important?
   a. To easily share it with friends and family
   b. To have a digital souvenir of your travels
   c. To safeguard against theft or loss and facilitate replacement
   d. To expedite passport renewal

Conclusion

As we reach the conclusion of "Essential Life Skills for Young Adults," take a moment to reflect on the valuable knowledge you've gained and the practical skills you've developed throughout this book. Our journey together has been dedicated to arming you with the essential life skills you'll need as you transition into adulthood, ready to tackle the diverse challenges and opportunities that await you.

Throughout these chapters, you've delved into a wide array of topics directly relevant to your life as a young adult. From understanding the intricacies of healthcare and wellness to navigating the complex terrain of relationships and sexual health, from mastering the art of social etiquette to becoming financially savvy, and from the intricacies of independent living to the digital landscape, mental health, and the critical aspects of managing essential documents and financial security – you've covered an extensive spectrum of indispensable life skills.

You've learned about the vital importance of health insurance, the keys to fostering healthy and meaningful relationships, the significance of budgeting and prudent money management, and the nuances of online etiquette. You've discovered how to maintain your physical and mental well-being, adapt seamlessly to independent living, and safeguard your essential documents and financial future.

As you conclude this transformative journey, remember that these skills are not mere theoretical concepts but rather practical tools that will serve you exceptionally well in various facets of your life. They are the cornerstones of your future success and overall well-being.

As you continue to progress and face new challenges, embracing opportunities along the way, rest assured that you now possess a solid foundation to navigate the complexities of adulthood. Keep the flames of curiosity and self-improvement burning brightly, continuing to apply these invaluable life skills to enrich not only your own life but also the lives of those around you.

This is not an end, but a fresh beginning, a new chapter in your journey. The knowledge you've acquired here is a potent instrument, and how you wield it will shape your future. Therefore, with unwavering confidence, resilience, and an unwavering commitment to seizing every opportunity that comes your way, step boldly into the next exciting phase of your life.

Congratulations on successfully completing this journey! Your future is luminous, and you are exceptionally well-prepared to meet it head-on with confidence and competence. Continue to flourish, persevere, and evolve into the best version of yourself. The world is yours to conquer, and you are more than ready for the challenge!

A SHINING OPPORTUNITY TO HELP ANOTHER YOUNG ADULT LIKE YOU!

We're thrilled you've chosen to dive into our book on essential life skills. Before you embark on this exciting journey through its pages, we want to invite you to be part of our community.

As you explore the wisdom and insights within these chapters, we encourage you to take your time, absorb the knowledge, and apply these skills to your life. We believe that your personal experiences with the content will make your review even more valuable.

If at any point in the book you have found it to be helpful, please consider leaving an honest review as we would love to hear your thoughts. Your honest review can help others understand how this book has impacted your life and what valuable lessons you've learned.

Remember, there's no rush! Whenever you feel inspired, consider sharing your review with us. Your feedback is invaluable and can inspire fellow readers on their own journeys.

Thank you for joining us in this adventure of personal growth and empowerment. We can't wait to hear your thoughts and insights as you explore the wealth of knowledge within these pages!

Leave a review for us!

Answer Key

Chapter 1

- ‣ Why is it important to have health insurance if you can?
    - Correct Answer: To protect yourself from high medical costs
- ‣ Why are wellness visits and preventive care important?
    - Correct Answer: They detect and prevent health issues early
- ‣ How can getting an estimate of cost help you?
    - Correct Answer: It allows you to plan your budget and make informed decisions
- ‣ How can you help keep your oral care healthy?
    - Correct Answer: All of the above.
- ‣ What is the difference between in and out-of-network?
    - Correct Answer: In-network providers have agreements with your insurance company, while out-of-network providers do not
- ‣ A fixed amount you pay for a service is called what?
    - Correct Answer: Co-pay

Chapter 2

- ‣ What is an essential aspect of cultivating healthy romantic relationships?
    - Correct Answer: Open and honest communication
- ‣ Why is it crucial to practice safe dating on dates?
    - Correct Answer: To ensure your safety
- ‣ What is an integral part of understanding sexual health?
    - Correct Answer: All of the above
- ‣ Which of the following is an example of an unhealthy romantic relationship?
    - Correct Answer: Emotional abuse and control
- ‣ What does consent mean in the context of sexual activity?

- Correct Answer: It encompasses clear communication, mutual agreement, and willingness from all parties involved.

Chapter 3

▸ What is one key purpose of etiquette in various scenarios?
  - Correct Answer: Demonstrating respect and consideration
▸ When attending a wedding, what are the proper etiquette guidelines to follow?
  - Correct Answer: Bring a gift even if you can't attend
▸ Why is tipping for dining, deliveries, and personal care important in various cultures and industries?
  - Correct Answer: All of the above
▸ What should you do when meeting someone's parents for the first time?
  - Correct Answer: All of the above.
▸ How can you express gratitude to service providers who offer exceptional service in the digital realm?
  - Correct Answer: Provide virtual tips or positive feedback

Chapter 4

▸ What is the primary purpose of creating a personal budget?
  - Correct Answer: To manage your income and expenses
▸ Why is it important to make on-time payments for your credit card bills?
  - Correct Answer: Because it helps build and maintain a positive credit history
▸ What is the significance of an emergency fund?
  - Correct Answer: It provides a financial safety net for unexpected expenses
▸ Which of the following is NOT a factor that affects your credit score?
  - Correct Answer: Your favorite color
▸ What is the recommended credit utilization ratio for maintaining a positive credit score?
  - Correct Answer: Below 30%

- ▸ Which of the following is NOT a step in balancing your checkbook?
  - • Correct Answer: Avoiding checking your bank statements
- ▸ Which of the following is NOT a strategy for managing debt?
  - • Correct Answer: Accumulating new debt regularly

Chapter 5

- ▸ When budgeting for rent, it's recommended not to spend more than what percentage of your monthly income?
  - • Correct Answer: 30%
- ▸ What should you consider when choosing an apartment location?
  - • Correct Answer: All of the above (The question implies multiple considerations are important, including proximity to work or school, noise level, etc.)
- ▸ Before signing a lease agreement, it's essential to carefully read and understand all the _____ to avoid any surprises later.
  - • Correct Answer: Terms and conditions (or clauses)
- ▸ Regular decluttering and creating a cleaning schedule helps in maintaining a _____ living space.
  - • Correct Answer: Organized and clean (or tidy)
- ▸ True or False: Emergency preparedness includes having a well-equipped emergency kit with essentials like non-perishable food and water.
  - • Correct Answer: True

Chapter 6

- ▸ What does HTTPS in a website URL indicate?
  - • Correct Answer: Highly Secure Encryption Protocol
- ▸ Which of the following is NOT a recommended practice for online privacy?
  - • Correct Answer: Conducting sensitive transactions on public Wi-Fi networks
- ▸ What is the purpose of Two-Factor Authentication (2FA)?
  - • Correct Answer: It adds an extra layer of security by requiring a second form of verification.

- When meeting sellers or buyers in person for transactions, it's important to choose _____, well-lit, and public locations.
  - Correct Answer: Safe (or secure)
- Leaving constructive feedback after an online transaction can help others make informed decisions. (True/False)
  - Correct Answer: True

Chapter 7

- Which of the following is NOT a common symptom of anxiety disorders?
  - Correct Answer: Persistent sadness
- Depression is often characterized by _____.
  - Correct Answer: A persistent feeling of sadness and hopelessness
- What is one effective way to manage stress and promote mental well-being?
  - Correct Answer: Practicing relaxation techniques like deep breathing and meditation
- A strong support network of friends and family can provide valuable _____ during difficult times.
  - Correct Answer: Emotional support (or support)
- Mental health is just as important as _____ health, and both should be prioritized for overall well-being.
  - Correct Answer: Physical

Chapter 8

- What is the primary purpose of a birth certificate?
  - Correct Answer: To confirm your identity and citizenship
- What should you do if you lose your Social Security card?
  - Correct Answer: Contact the Social Security Administration and follow their replacement process
- Why is maintaining a digital backup of your passport important?
  - Correct Answer: To safeguard against theft or loss and facilitate replacement

References

ARRICCA ELIN SANSONE, EMY RODRIGUEZ FLORES. (2019, Dec 20). *50+ Little Social Etiquette Rules Everyone Should Follow.* Retrieved from Country Living: https://www.countryliving.com/life/g15915245/social-etiquette/

Armenia, U. (2022, April 25). *Dispelling Myths and Misconceptions About Vaccines.* Retrieved from UNICEF Armenia: https://www.unicef.org/armenia/en/stories/dispelling-myths-and-misconceptions-about-vaccines

BLOG, F. (2021, Feb 01). *Car Safety Tips EVERY College Student Should Know.* Retrieved from Feed that Nation: https://feedthatnation.com/car-safety-tips-every-college-student-should-know/

Cambria. (2023, February 22). *The Importance of Financial Literacy for College Students.* Retrieved from Cambria: https://cambriaschool.com/blog/the-importance-of-financial-literacy-for-college-students/

Christine Frank, D. (2019, March 8). *Everything You Need to Know About Dental and Oral Health.* Retrieved from Healthline: https://www.healthline.com/health/dental-and-oral-health#_noHeaderPrefixedContent

Egan, J. (2023, Nov 7). *How to Balance a Checkbook.* Retrieved from U.S.News: https://www.usnews.com/banking/articles/how-to-balance-a-checkbook

Elizabeth Davis, RN . (2023, Dec 17). *HMO, PPO, EPO, POS–Which Plan Should You Choose?* Retrieved from VeryWell health: https://www.verywellhealth.com/hmo-ppo-epo-pos-whats-the-difference-1738615

Filaski, C. (2022, April 26). *7 things to know when cooking as a college student.* Retrieved from Cougarbuzz: https://cougarbuzz.com/2022/04/26/7-things-to-know-when-cooking-as-a-college-student/

Hopkins, J. (n.d.). *Medication Management and Safety Tips.* Retrieved from Johns Hopkins: https://www.hopkinsmedicine.org/health/wellness-and-prevention/help-for-managing-multiple-medications

Jensen, M. (2023, Oct 3). *How to Schedule Appointments With Your Patients? 12 Proven Strategies.* Retrieved from DemandHub: https://www.demandhub.co/articles/patient-appointment-scheduling/

Kovacs, K. (2022, Nov 23). *Understanding Sexual Health in College.* Retrieved from Best Colleges: https://www.bestcolleges.com/resources/sexual-health/

M, A. K. (n.d.). *What are the most effective ways to teach digital literacy and online safety?* Retrieved from LinkedIn: https://www.linkedin.com/advice/0/what-most-effective-ways-teach-digital-literacy

Maheshwari, R. (2023, Dec 27). *What Is Health Insurance: Meaning, Benefits & Types.* Retrieved from forbes: https://www.forbes.com/advisor/in/health-insurance/what-is-health-insurance/

Meyers, J. (2022, April 01). *10 tips to help you find the perfect apartment after college.* Retrieved from CNBC: https://www.cnbc.com/2022/04/01/10-tips-to-help-you-find-the-perfect-apartment-after-college.html

RAINN. (n.d.). *Online Dating and Dating App Safety Tips.* Retrieved from RAINN: https://www.rainn.org/articles/online-dating-and-dating-app-safety-tips

Ramsey. (2023, Dec 8). *How to Organize Your Important Documents.* Retrieved from RAMSEY: https://www.ramseysolutions.com/retirement/organizing-your-important-documents

Ravenscraft, E. (2020, Jan 23). *An Adult's Guide to Social Skills, for Those Who Were Never Taught.* Retrieved from The New York Times: https://www.nytimes.com/2020/01/23/smarter-living/adults-guide-to-social-skills.html

Team, A. A. (2022, April 12). *Digital Literacy in 2023.* Retrieved from Academy: https://www.avast.com/c-digital-literacy

Vadnal, J. (2023, February 2). *The Ultimate Guide to Tipping Etiquette in Every Situation—and When Not to Tip.* Retrieved from Real Simple: https://www.realsimple.com/work-life/money/money-etiquette/tipping-etiquette-guide

Vaghefi, S. (2023, May 09). *Etiquette Definition, Types & Rules.* Retrieved from Study.com : https://study.com/academy/lesson/etiquette-definition-types-rules.html

WPShealth. (n.d.). *Health Insurance Terminology and Definitions.* Retrieved from WPShealth: https://www.wpshealth.com/resources/customer-resources/health-insurance-terminology.shtml

Young, E. (2022, Jul 15). *Mental Health in College: Why It's Important and What You Can Do.* Retrieved from Admisions.usf: https://admissions.usf.edu/blog/mental-health-in-college-why-its-important-and-what-you-can-do

Zubair, M. (2023, Oct 29). *The Importance of Financial Literacy for Young Adults.* Retrieved from Medium: https://medium.com/@MuhammadZubairMalik/the-importance-of-financial-literacy-for-young-adults-21d34a011339

Made in the USA
Middletown, DE
16 November 2024

64705028R00092